Compassion for animals has no nationality. Wherever an animal is suffering, there my soul will be. I have no nationality, I have love and compassion for all forms of life."Amara Antara

LEIF SANDER NENEMANN

2024

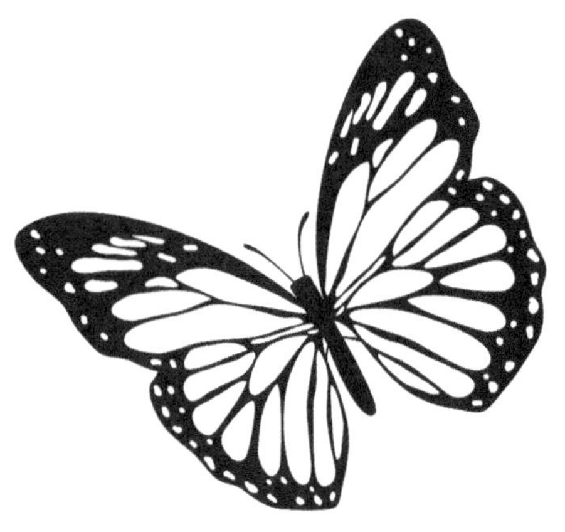
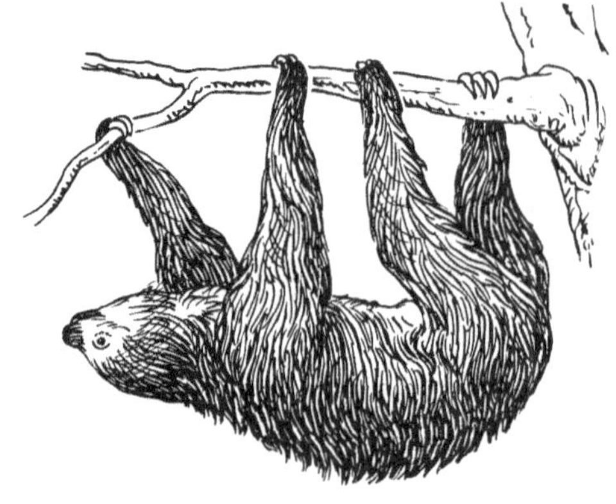

This Book Belongs to:

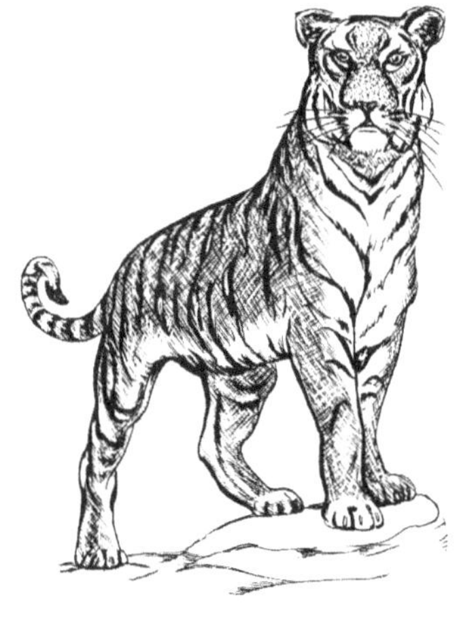
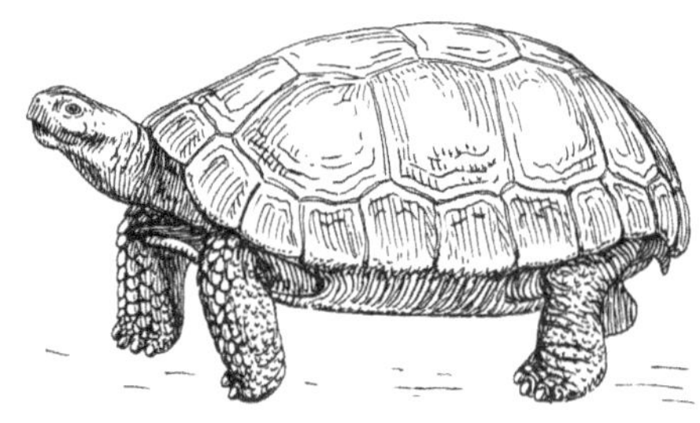

Test Color Page

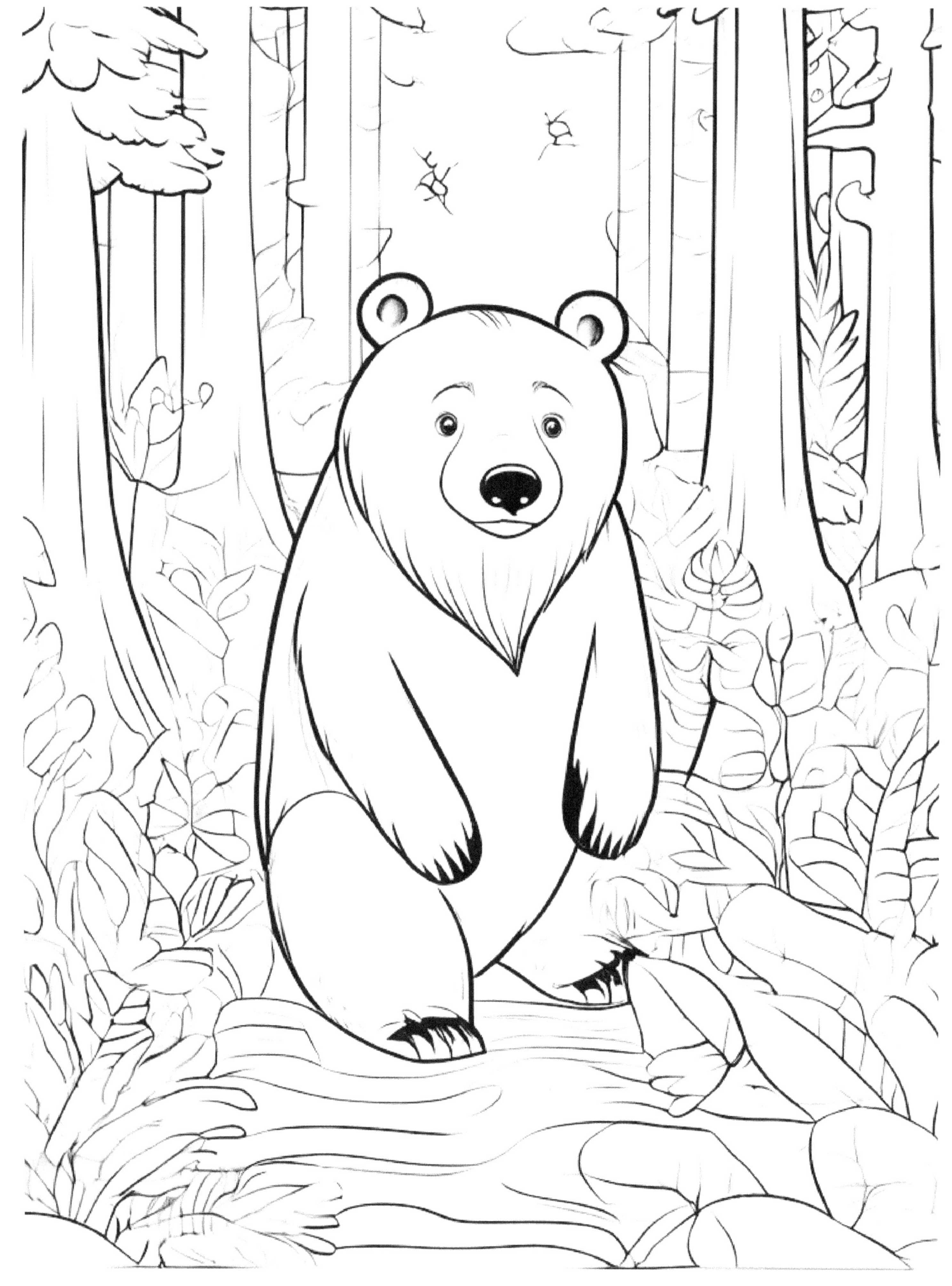

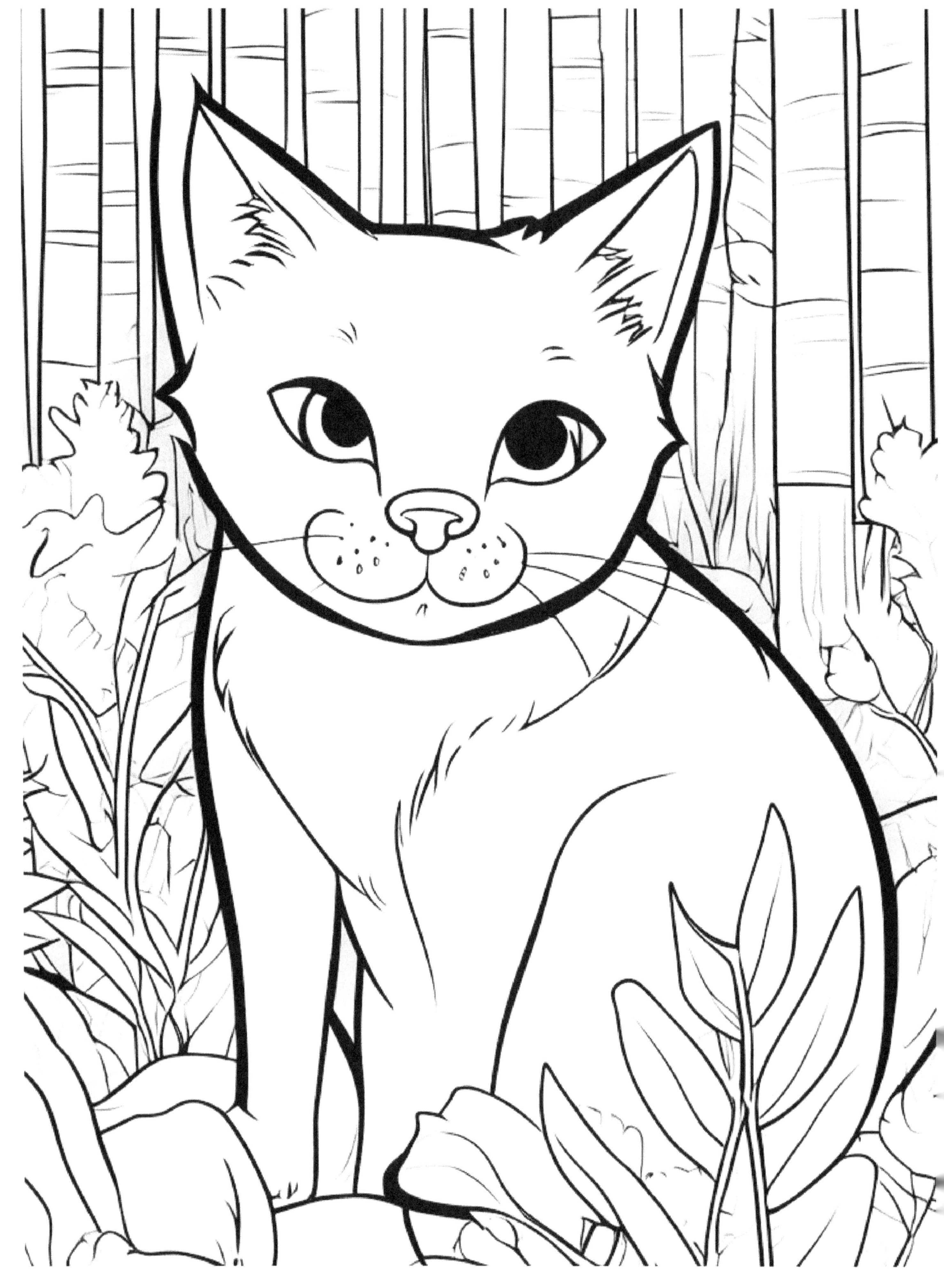

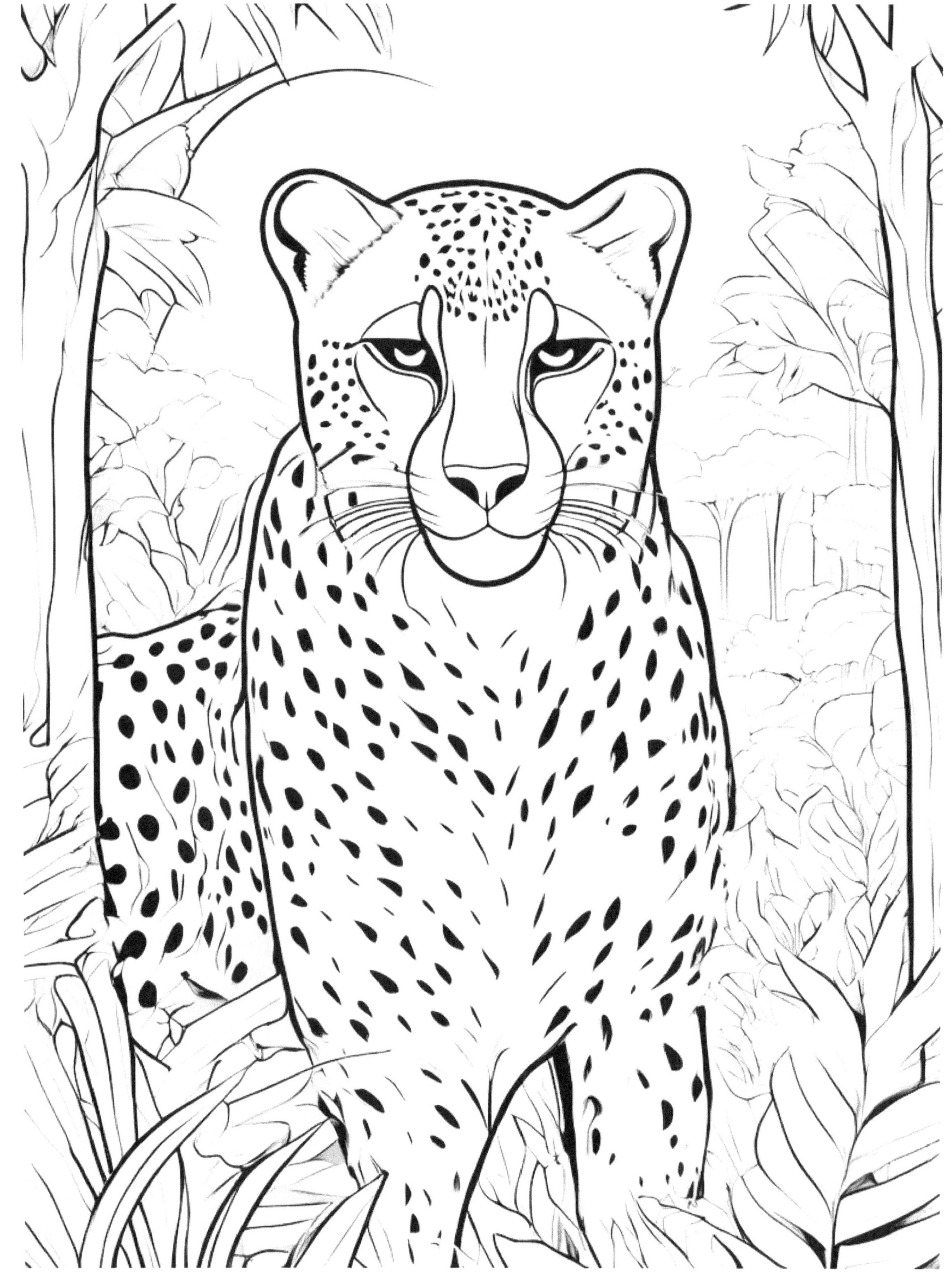

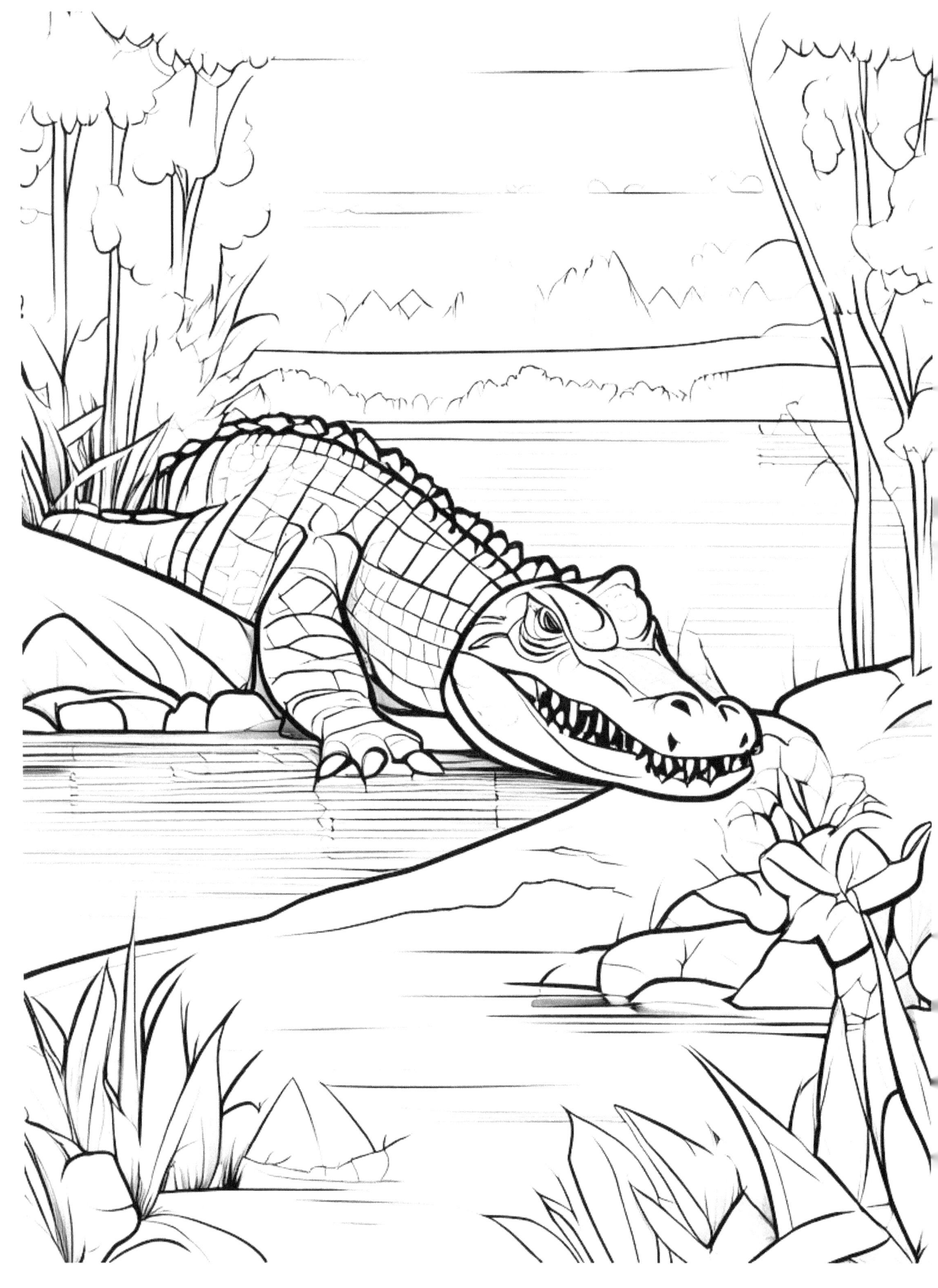

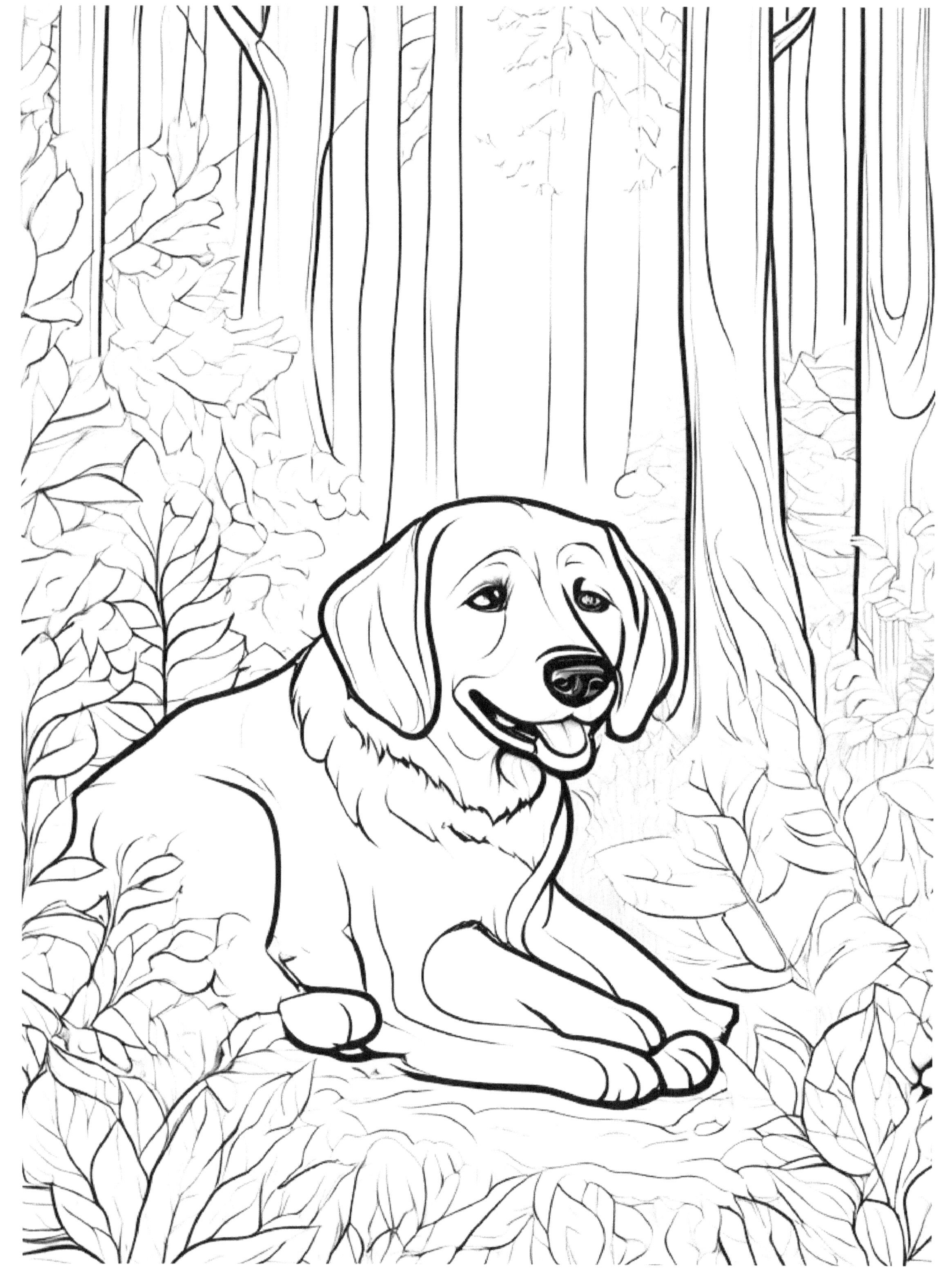

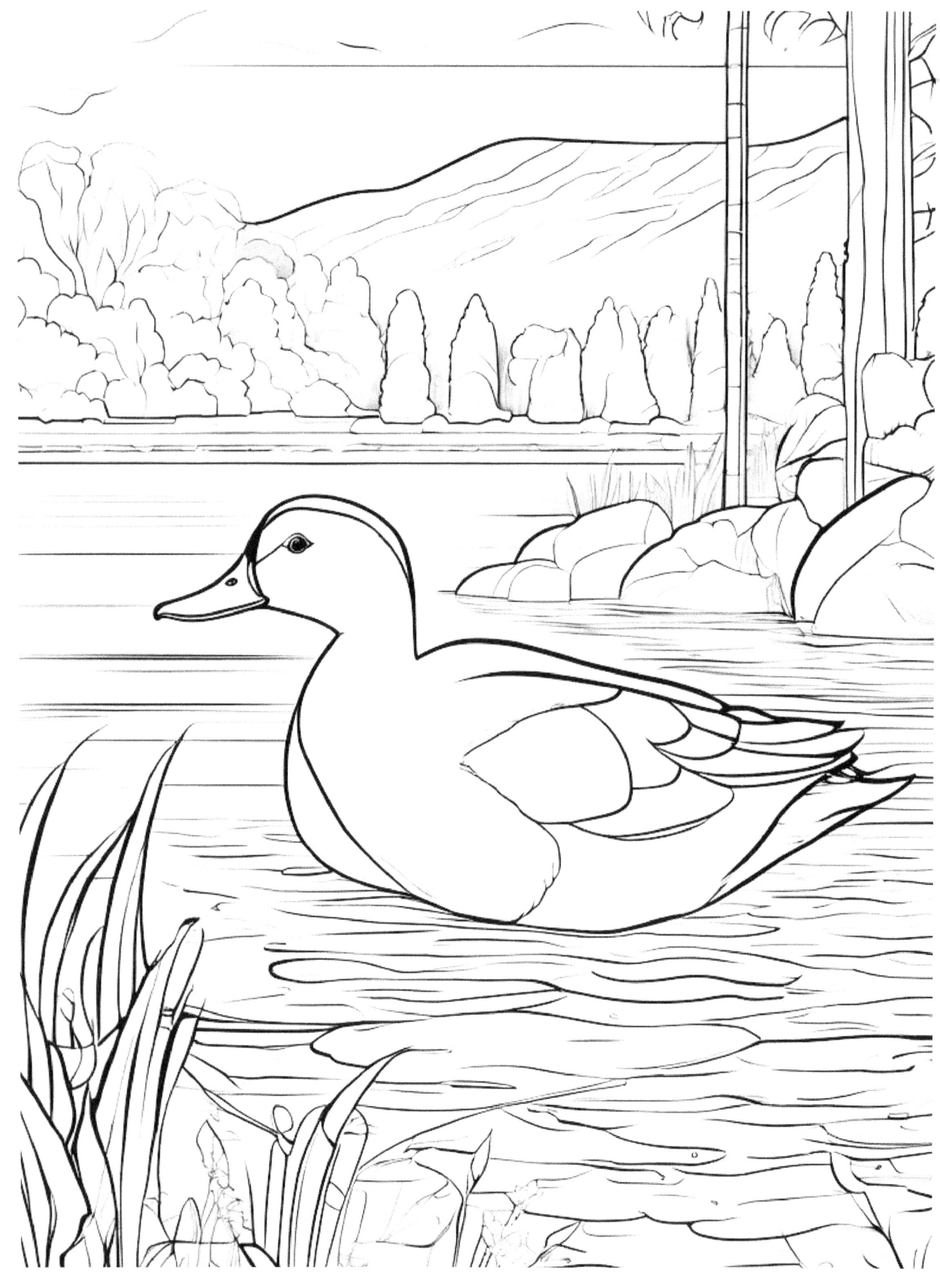

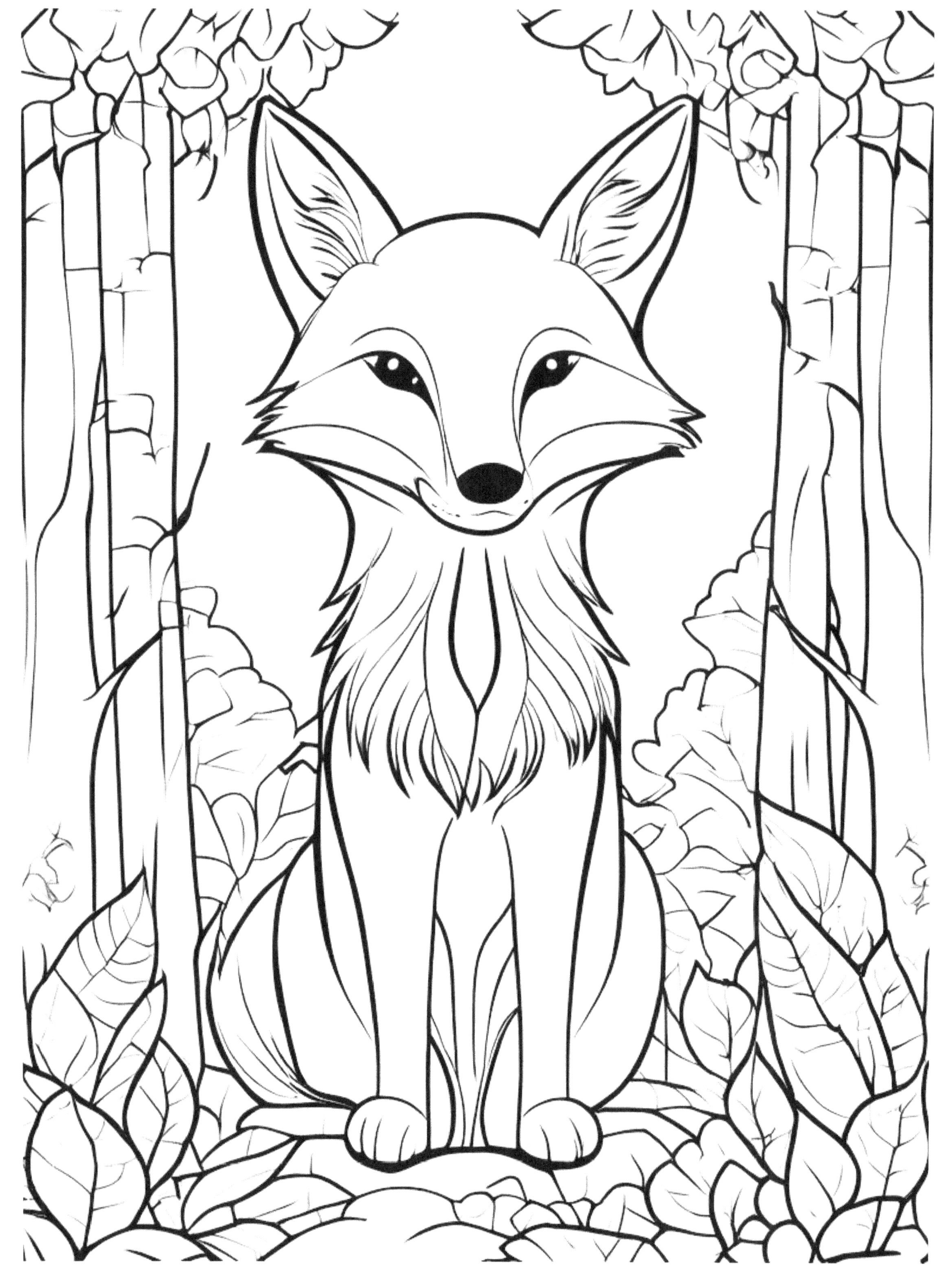

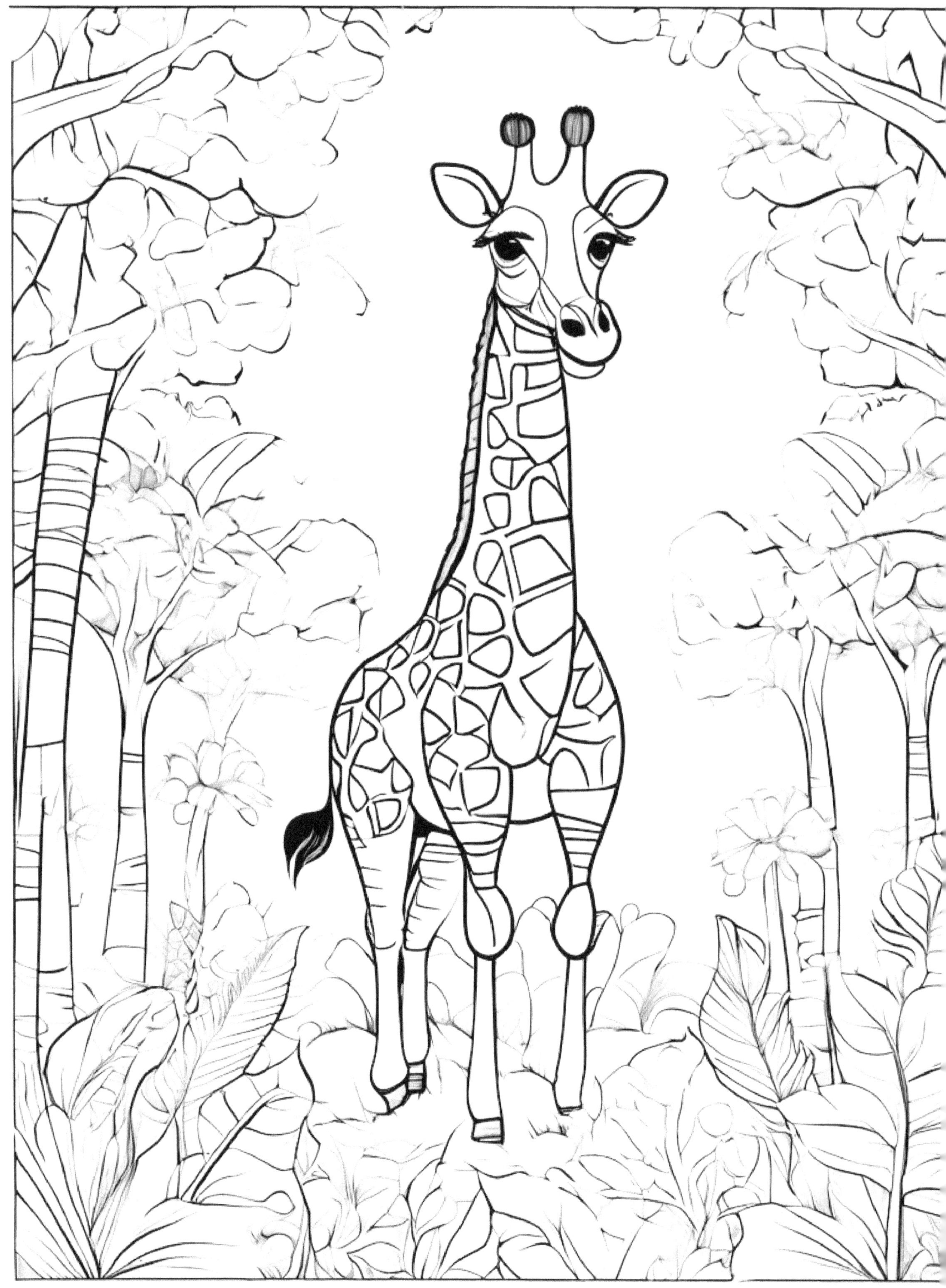

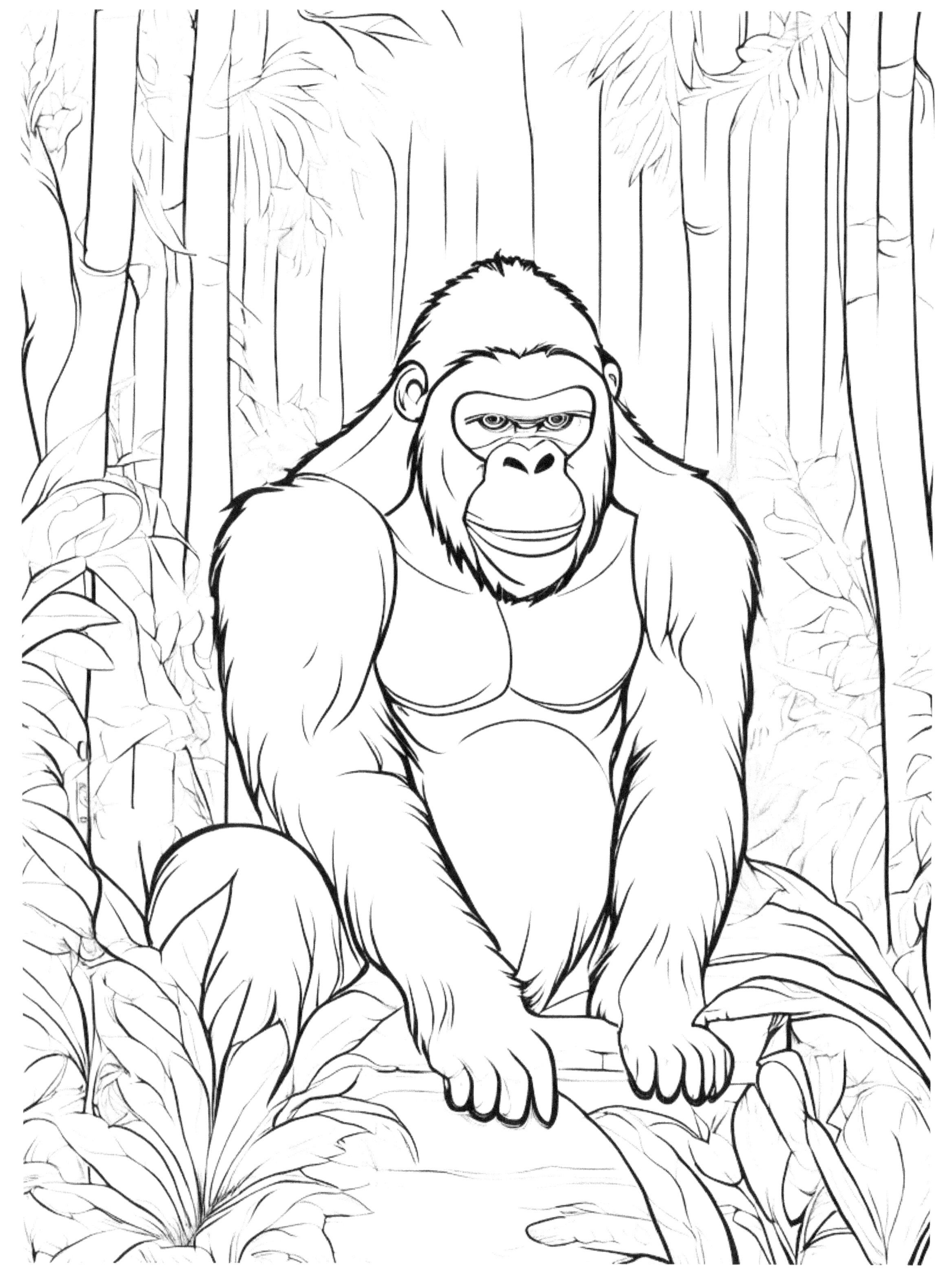

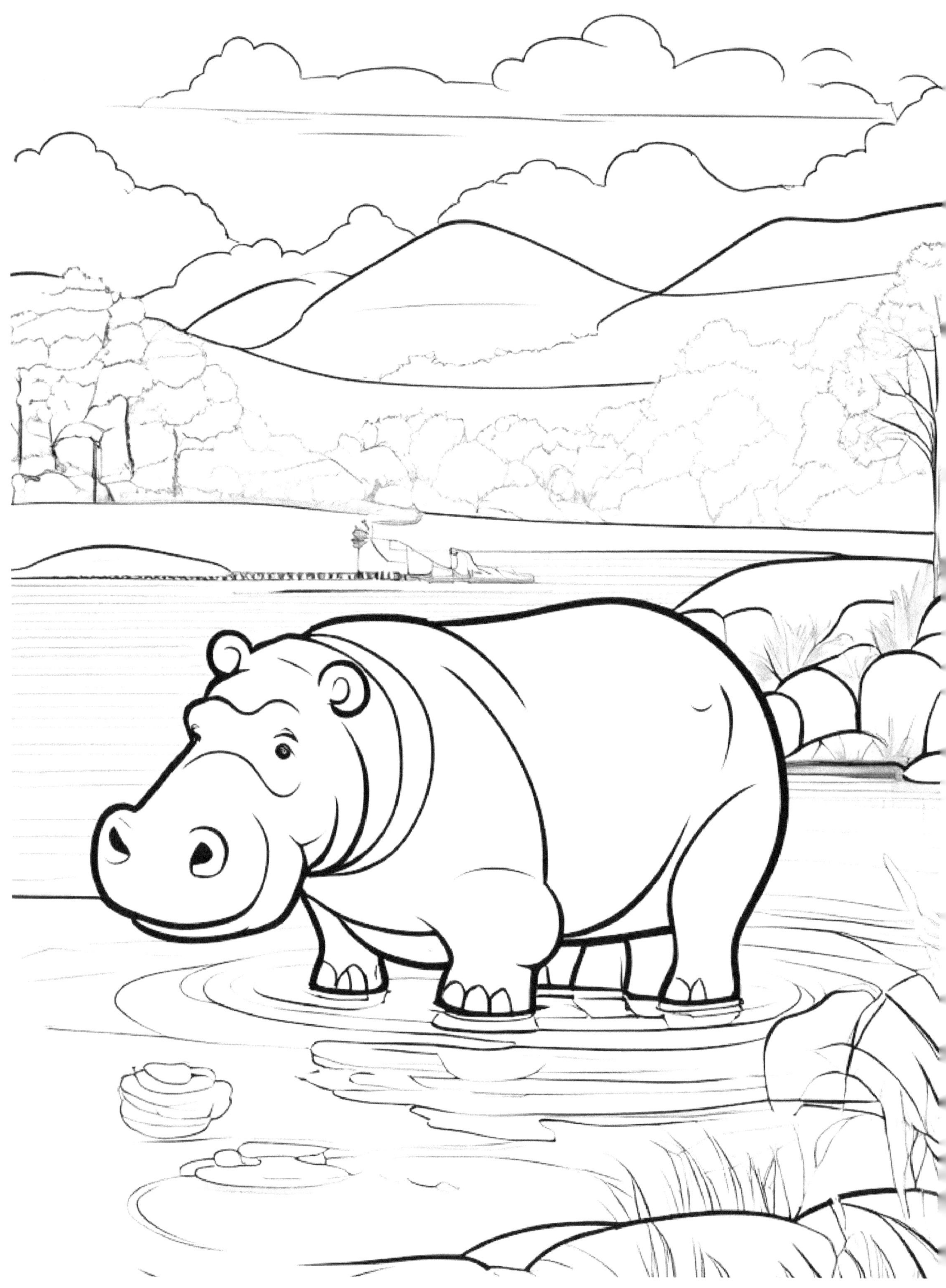

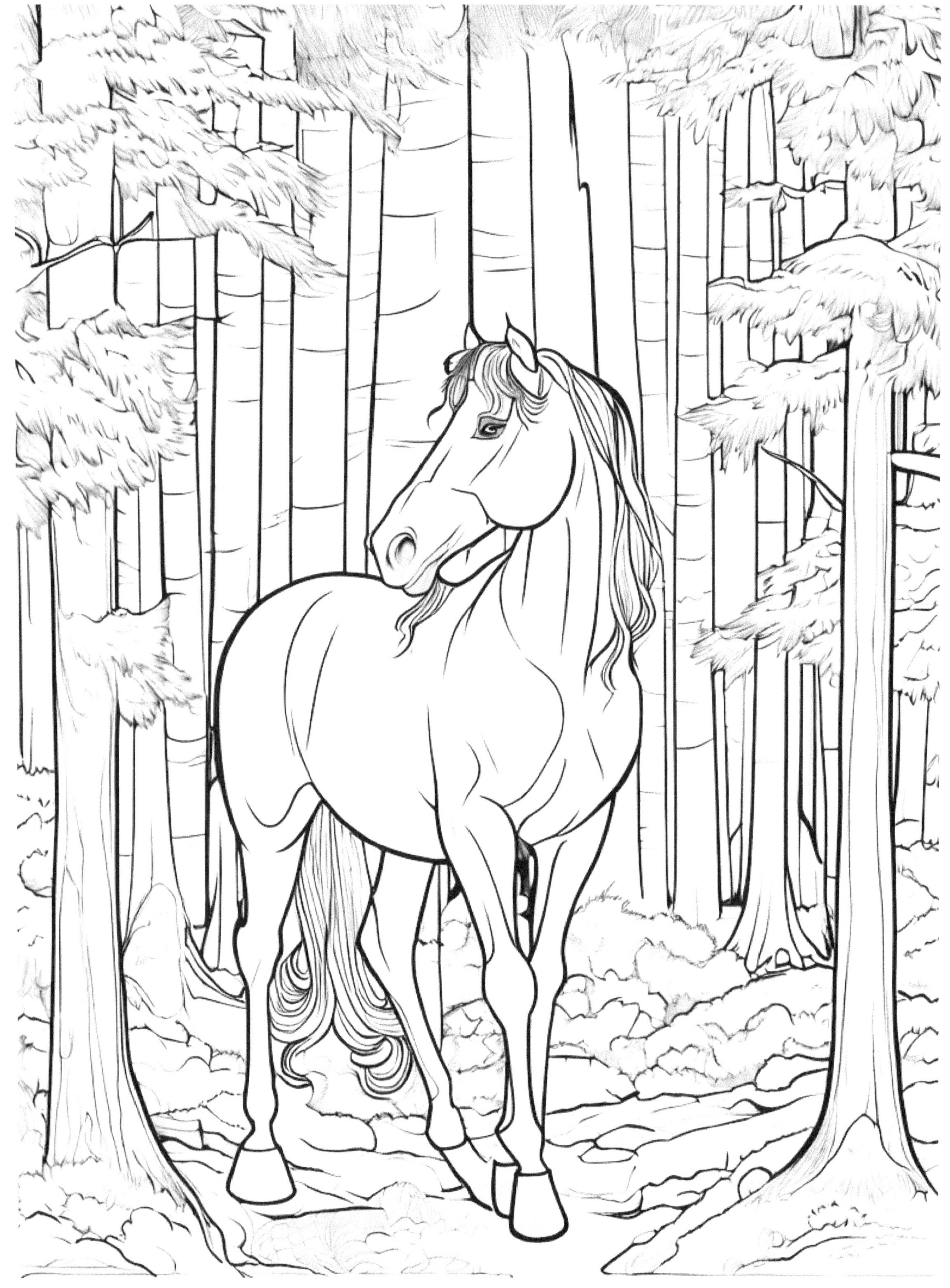

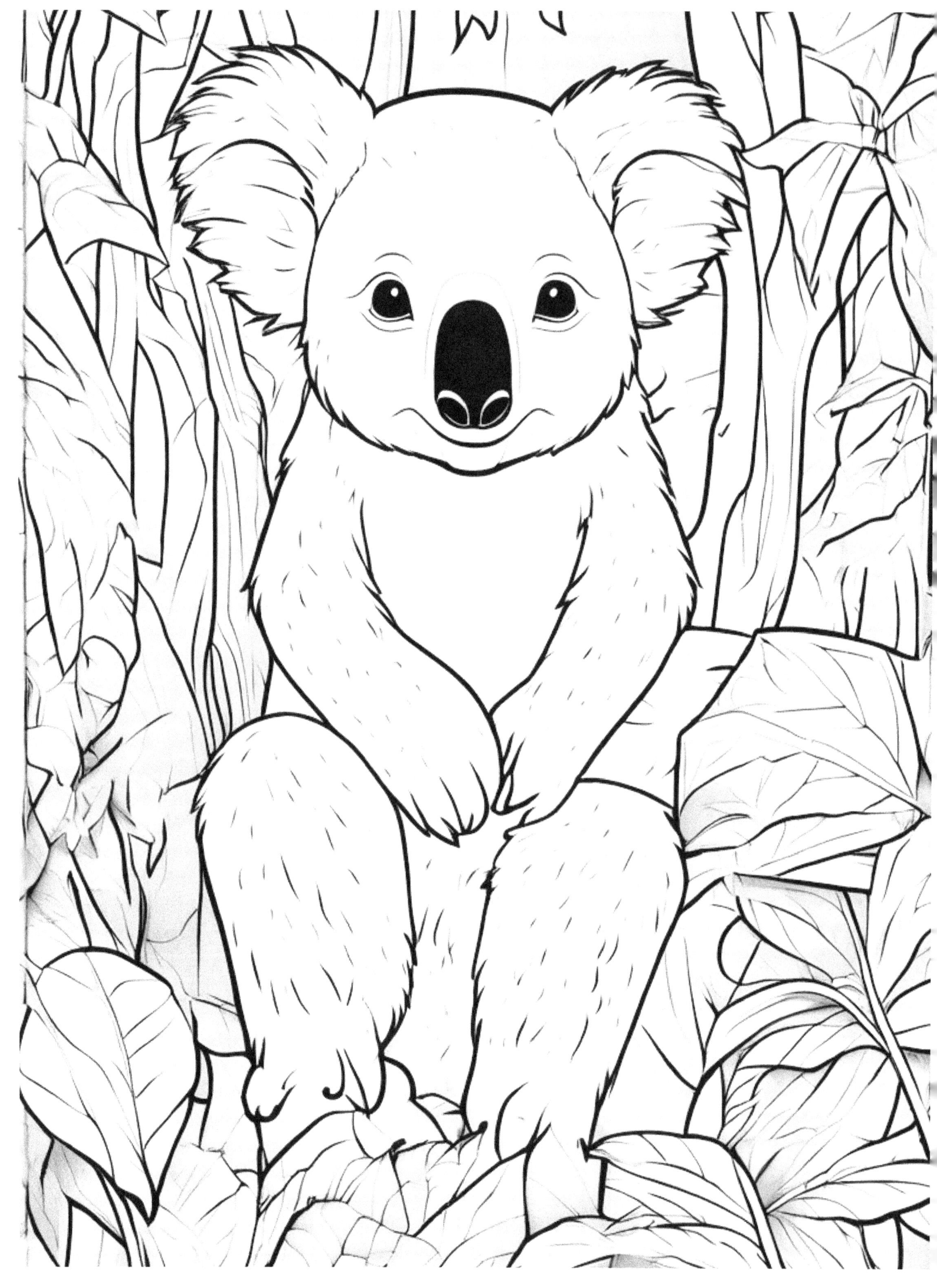

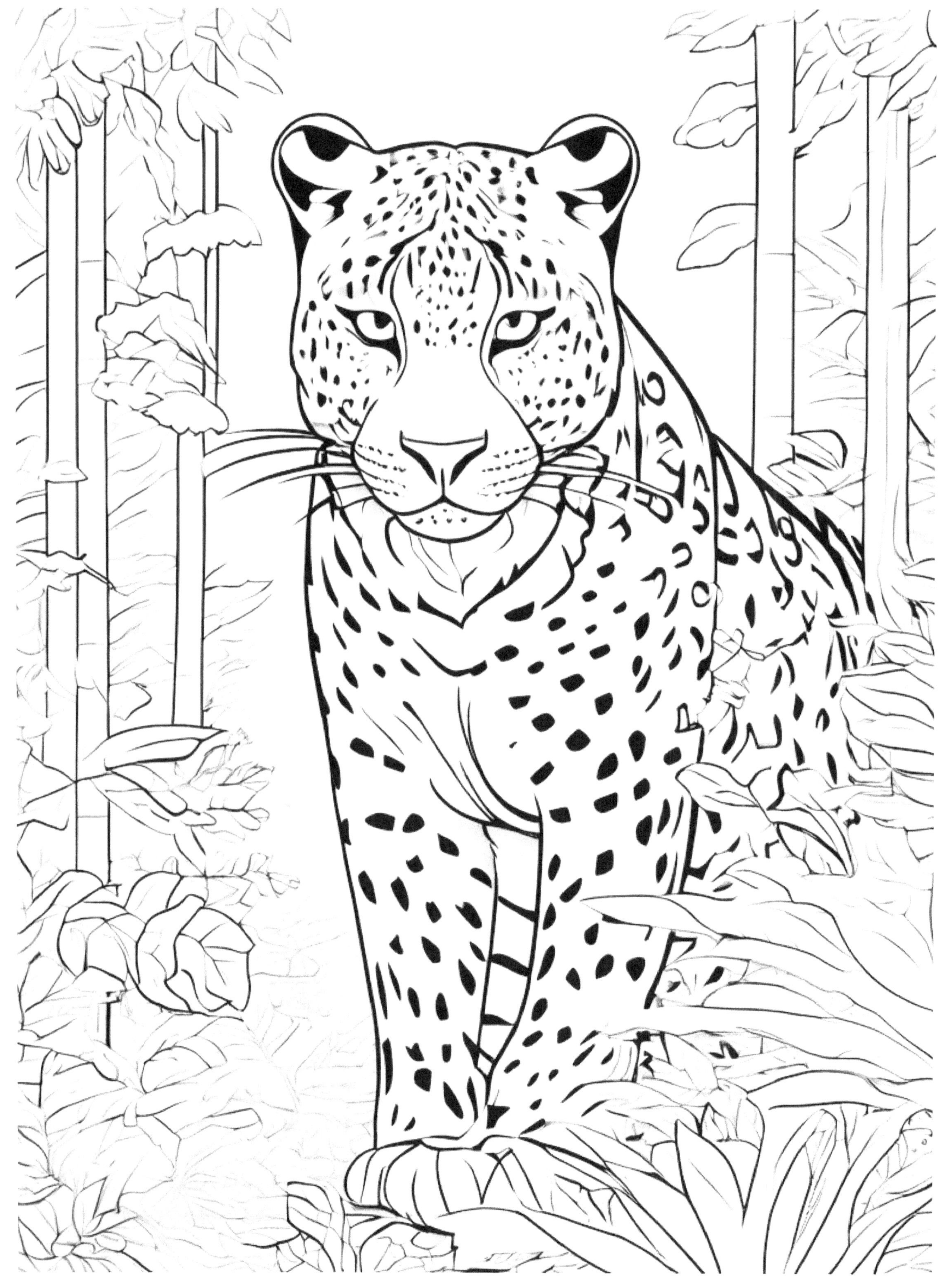

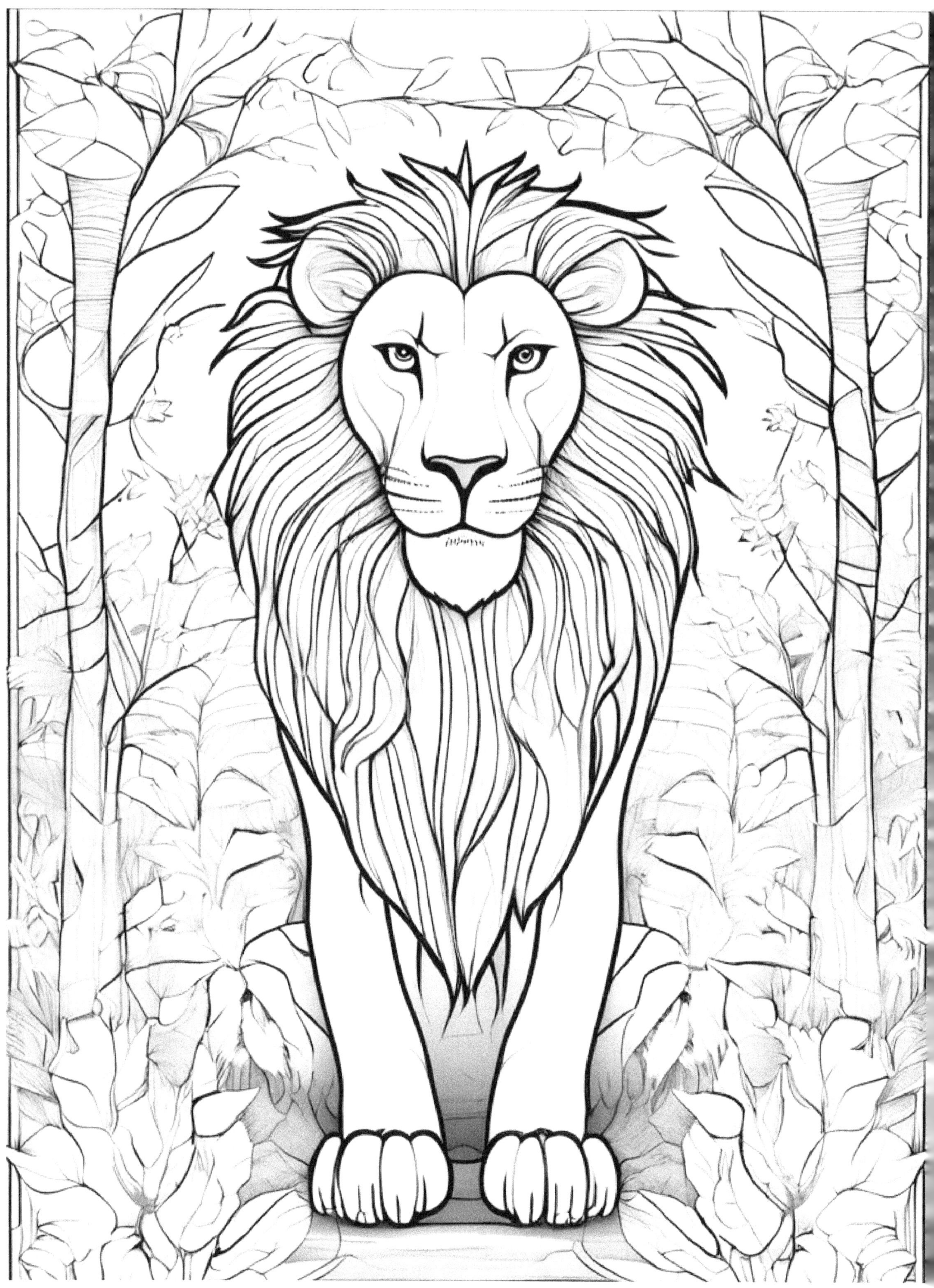

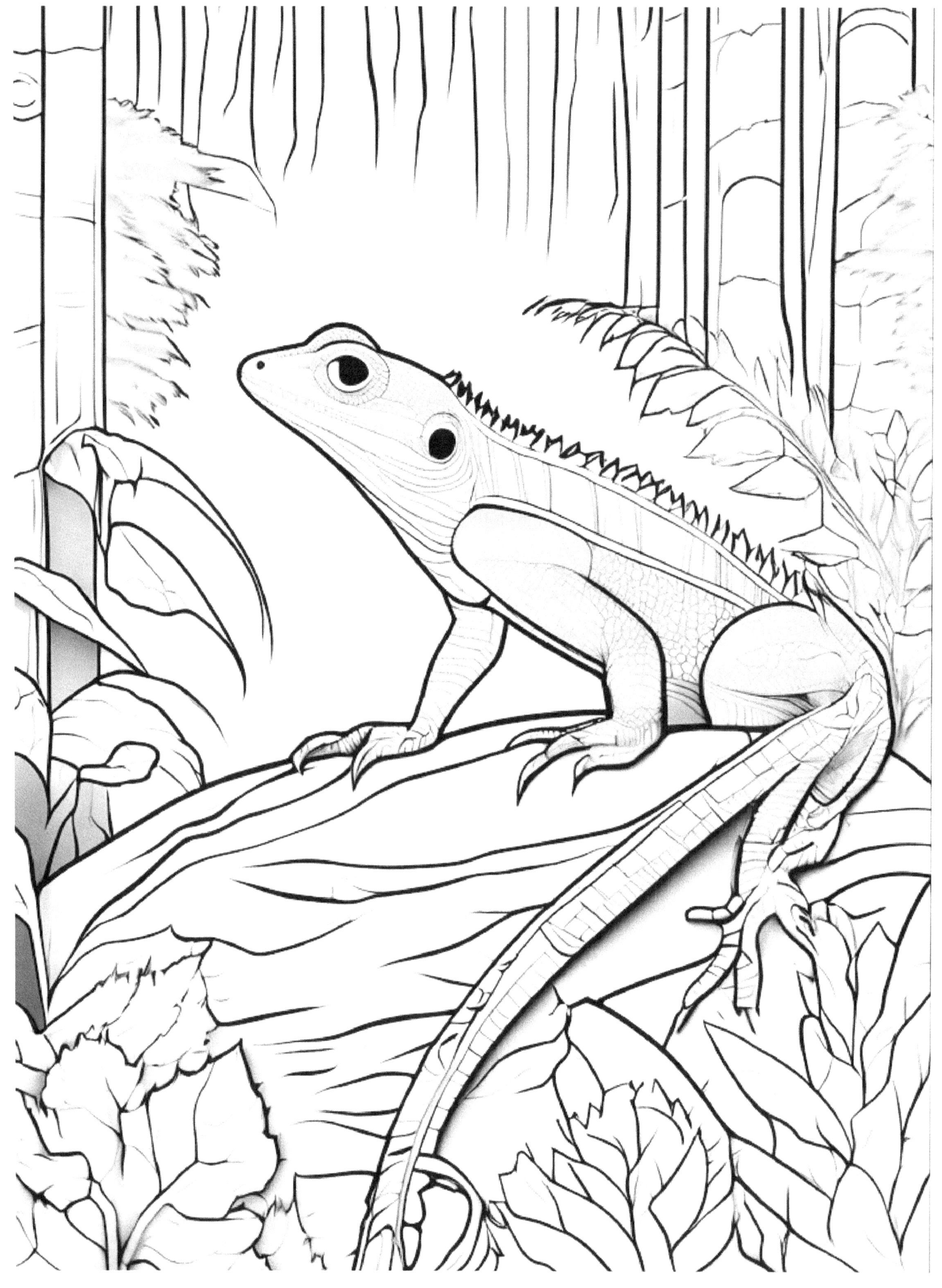

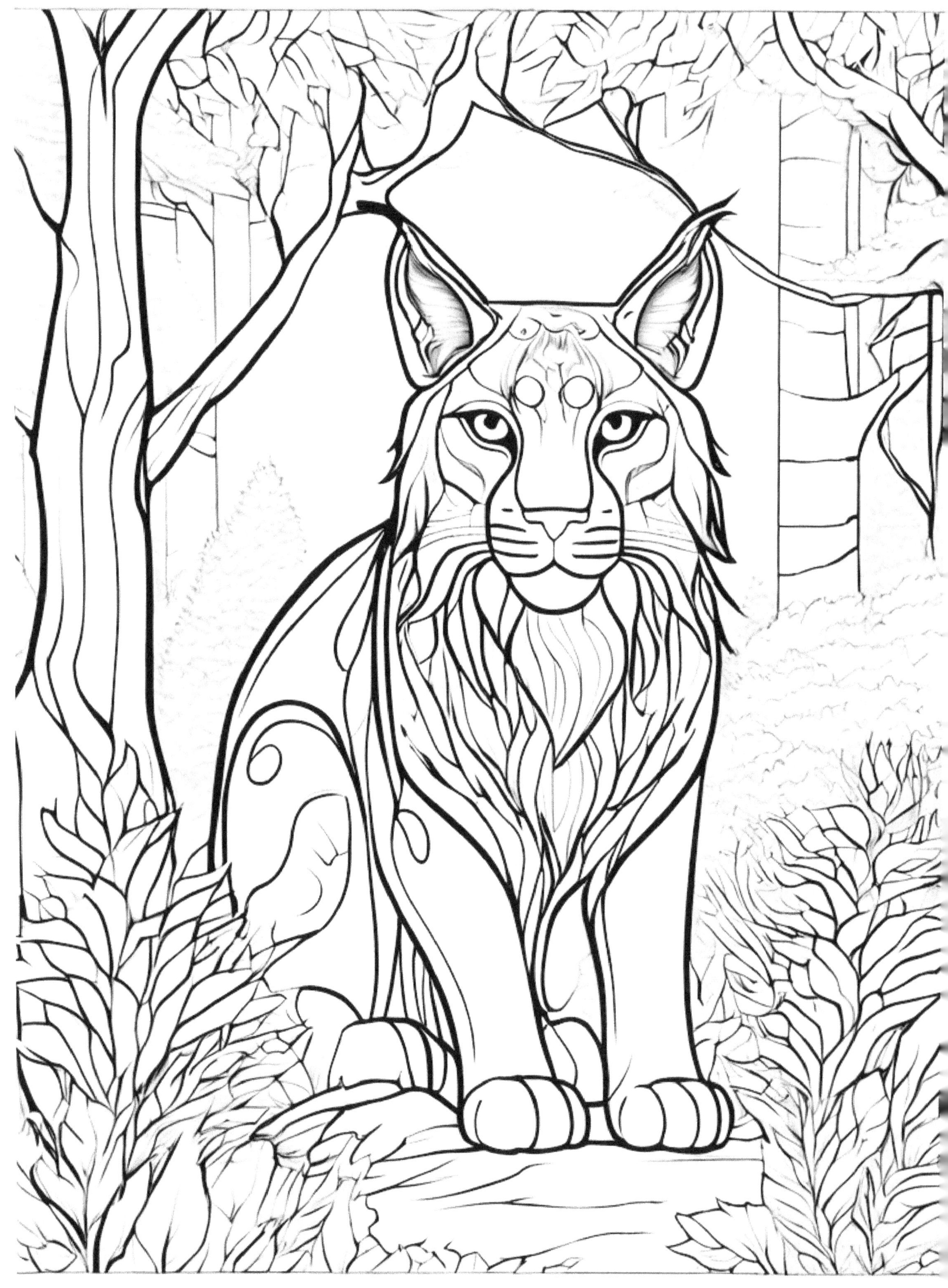

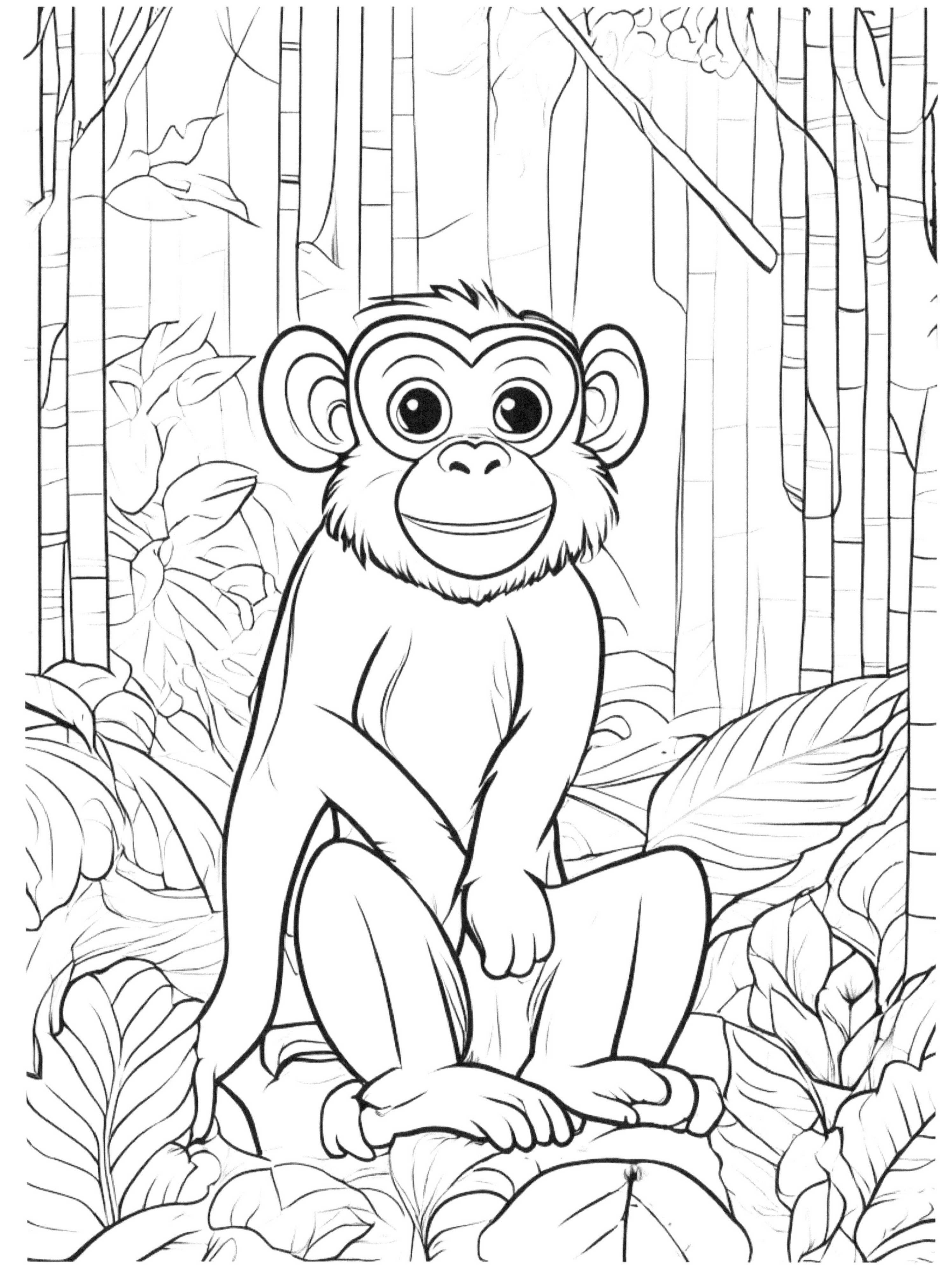

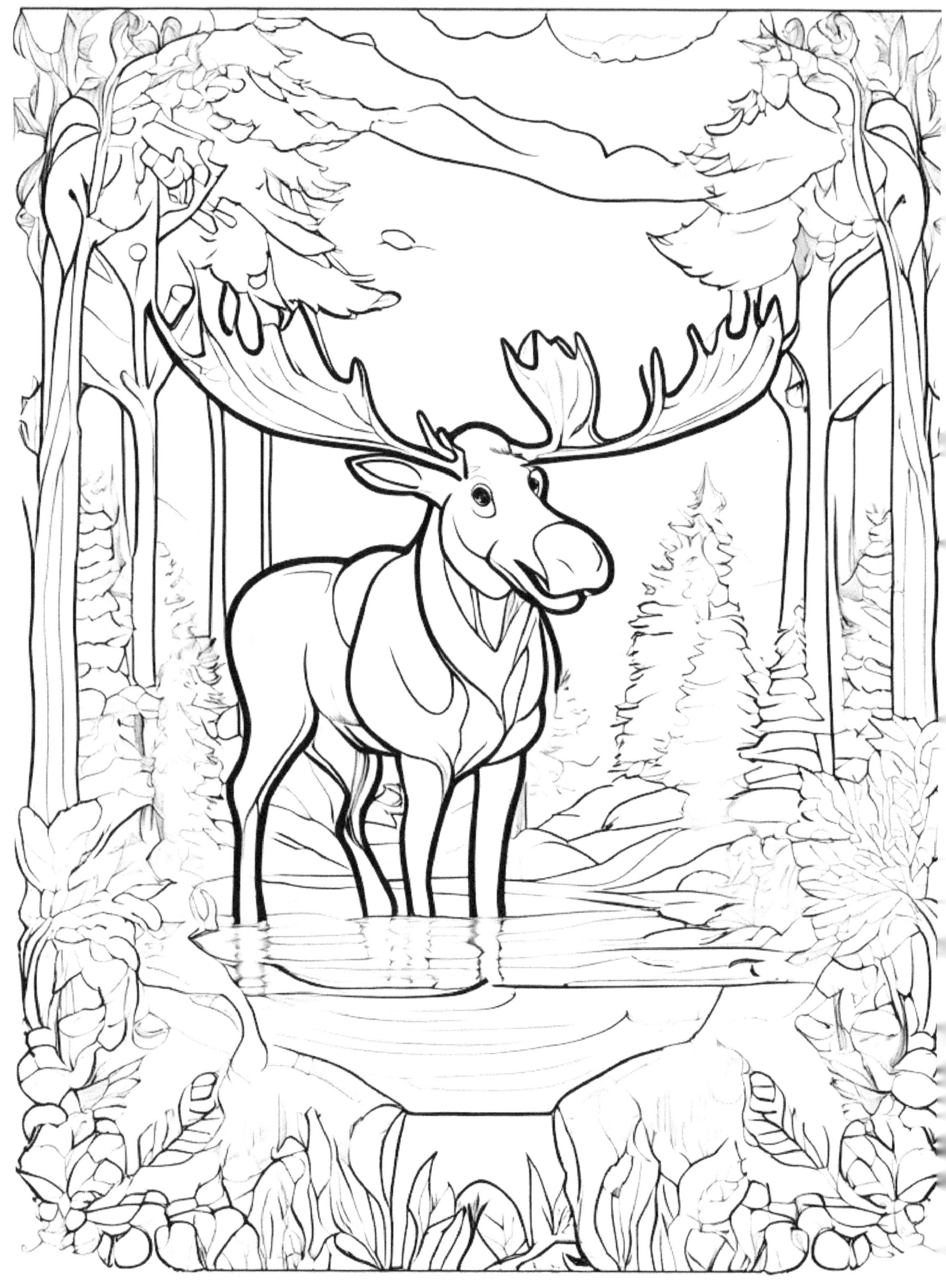

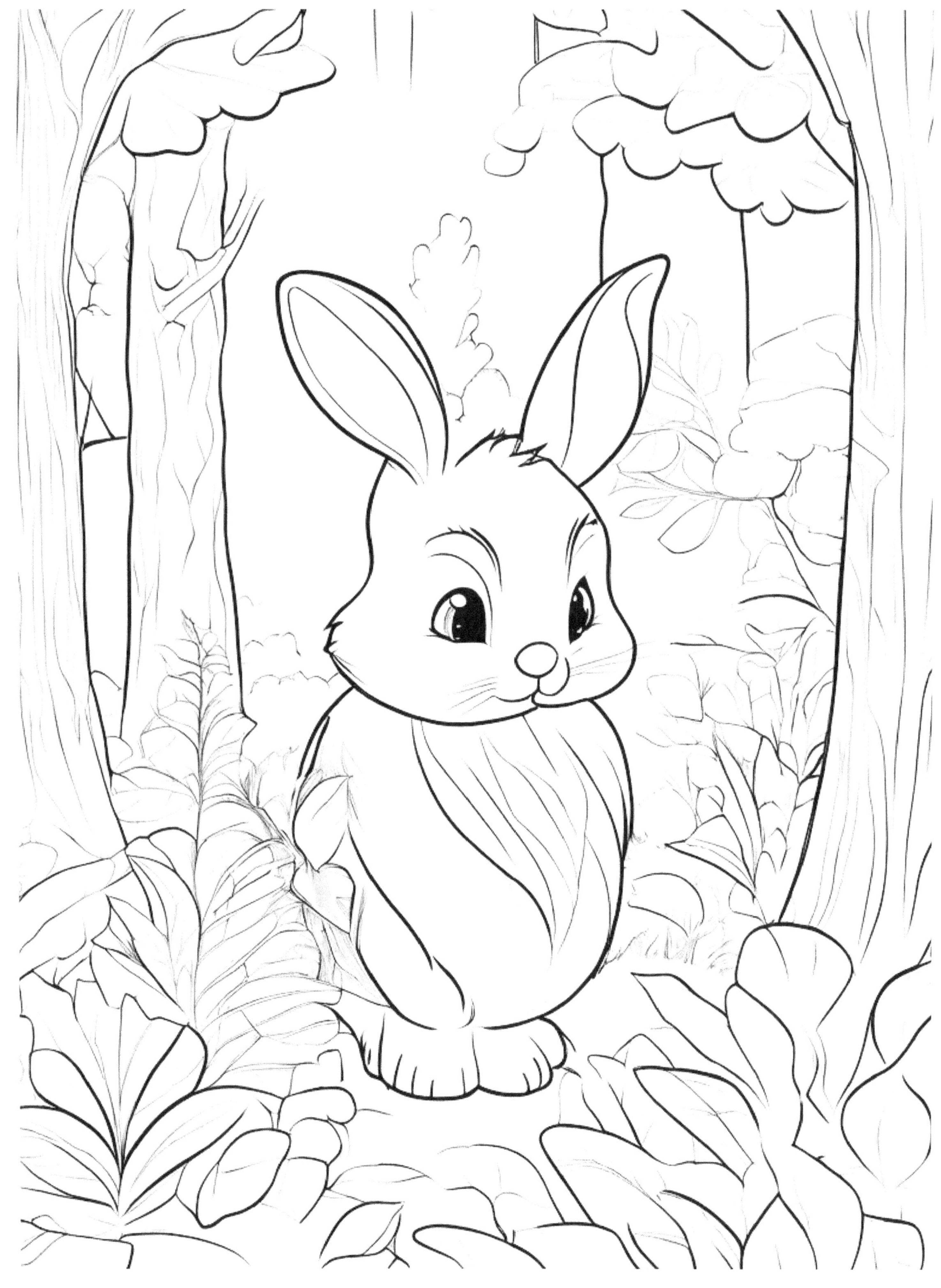

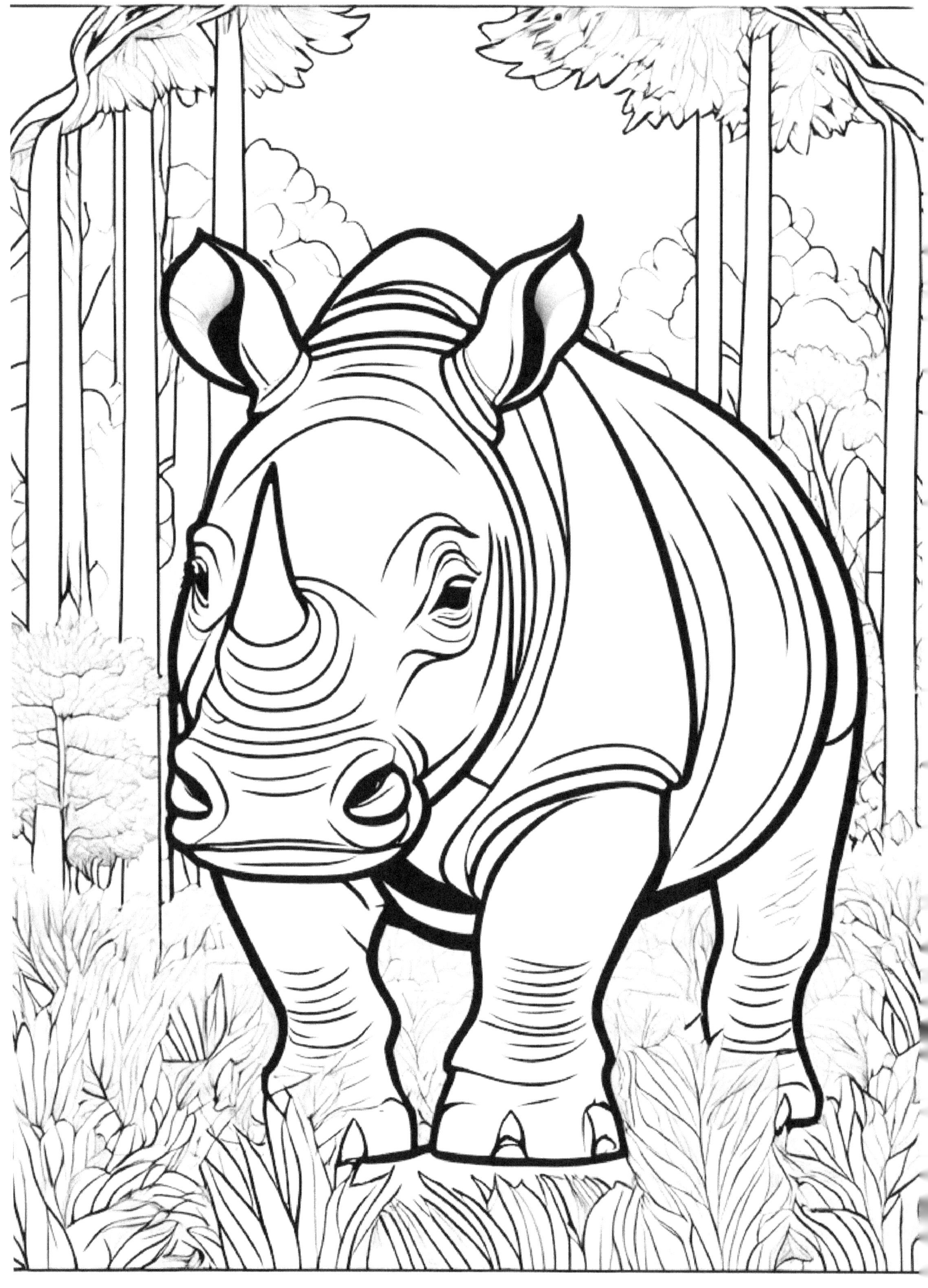

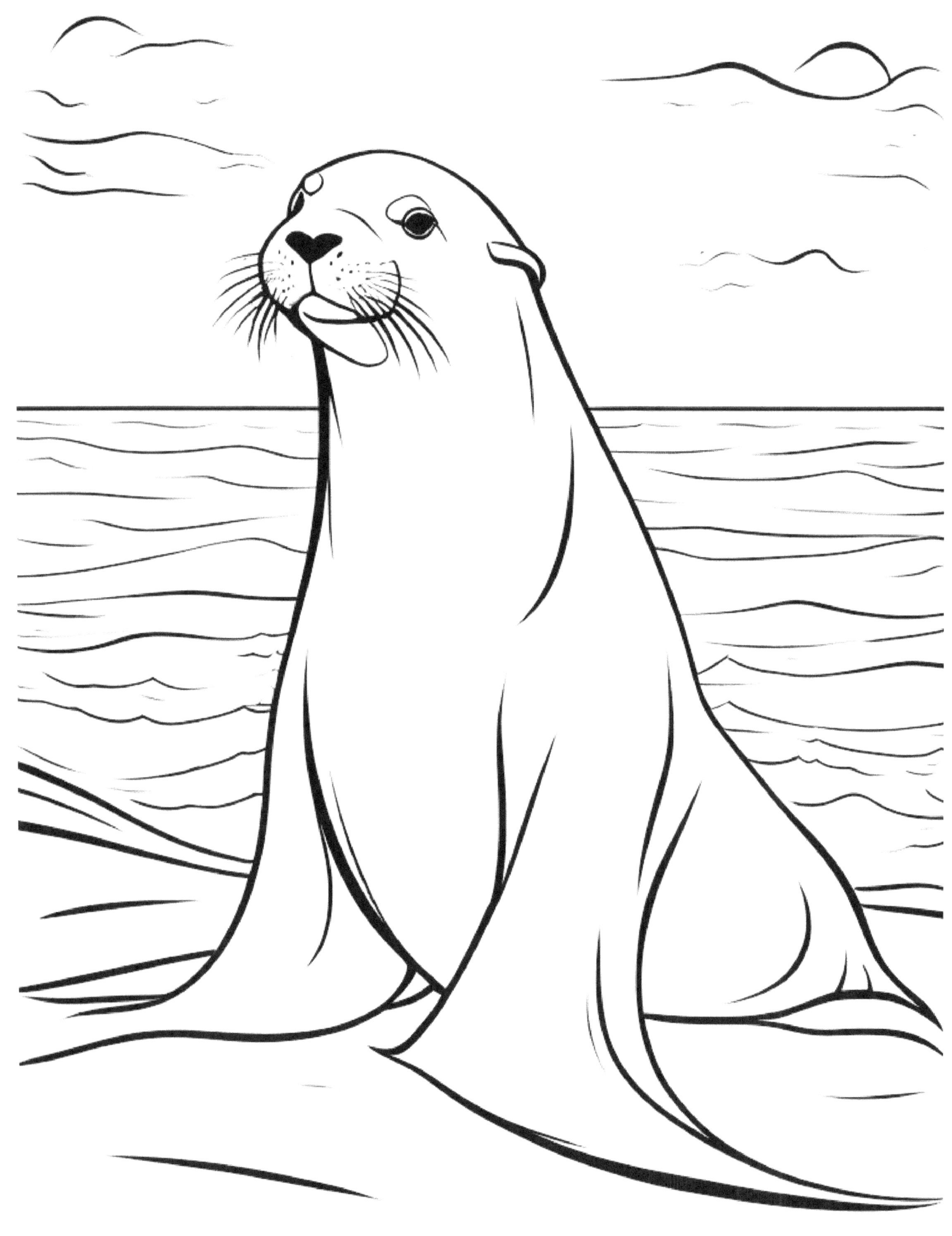

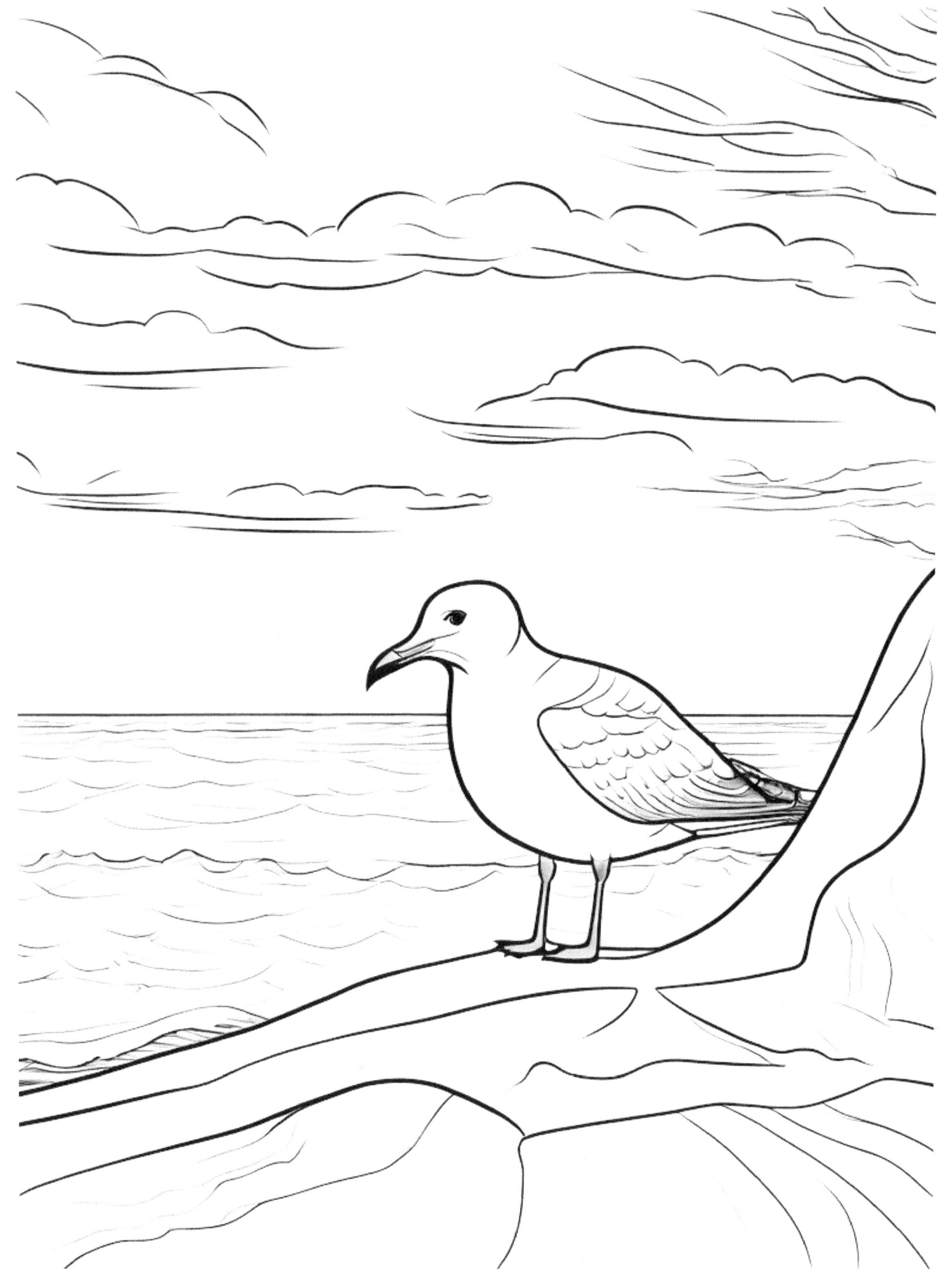

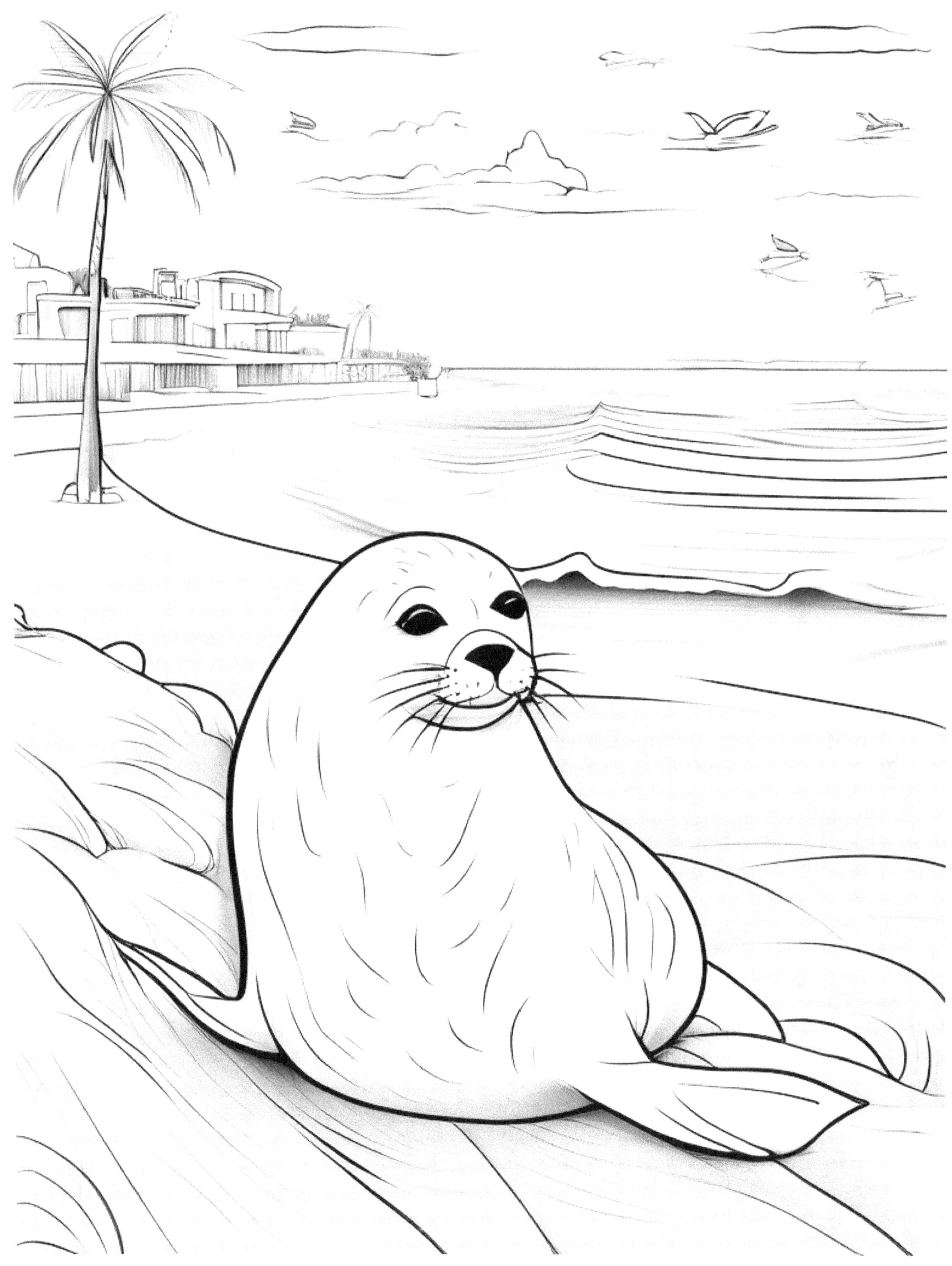

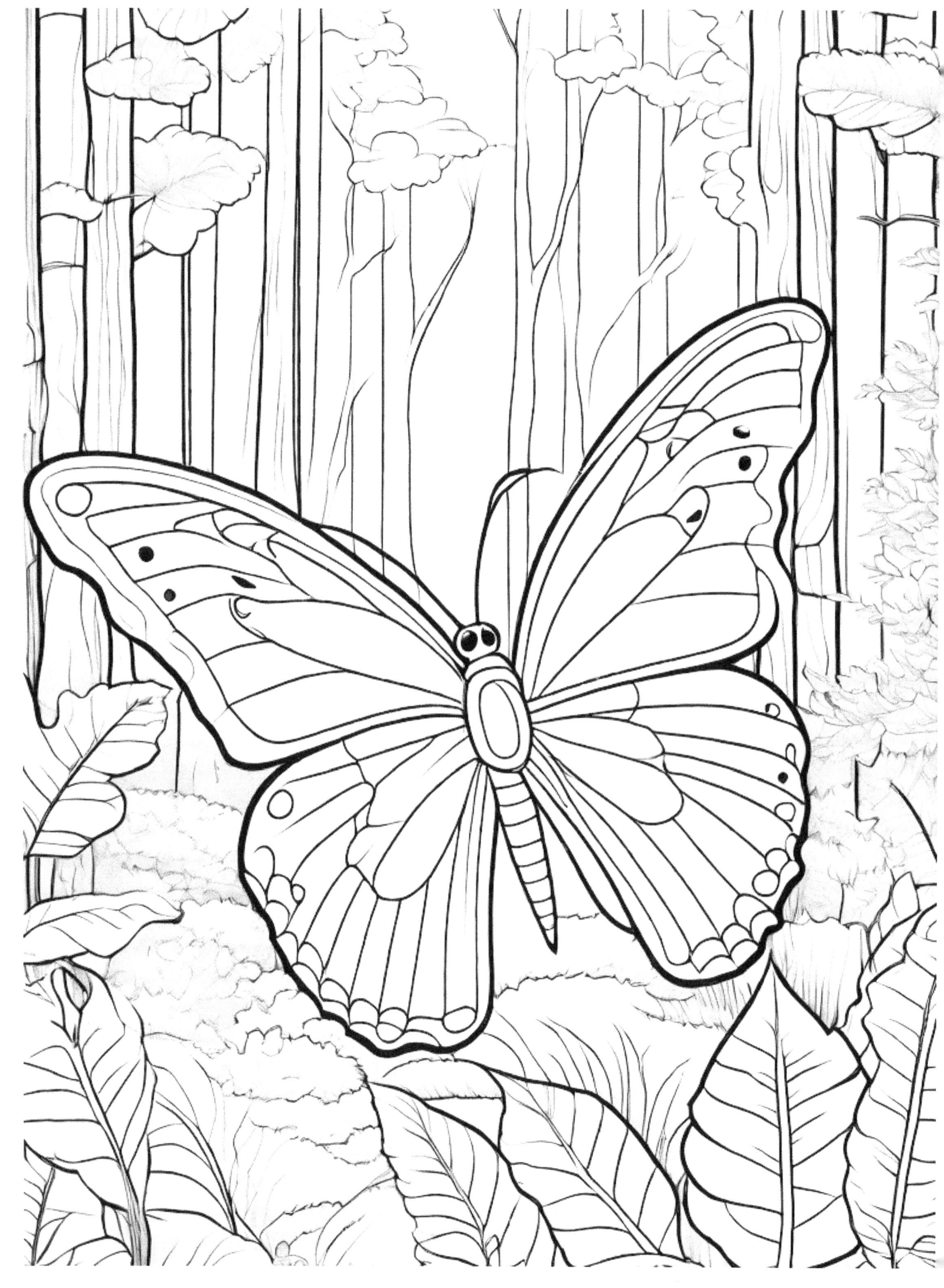

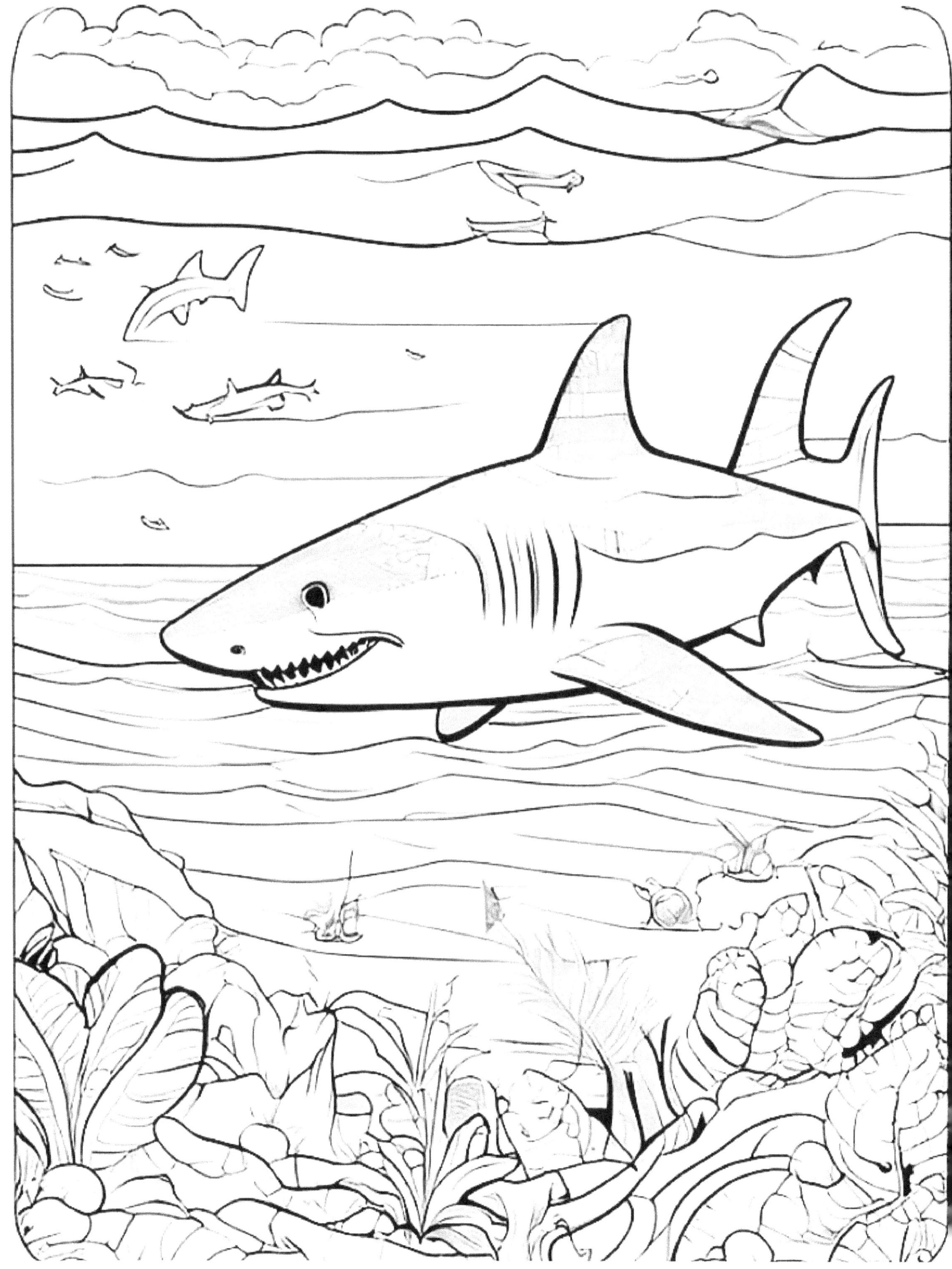

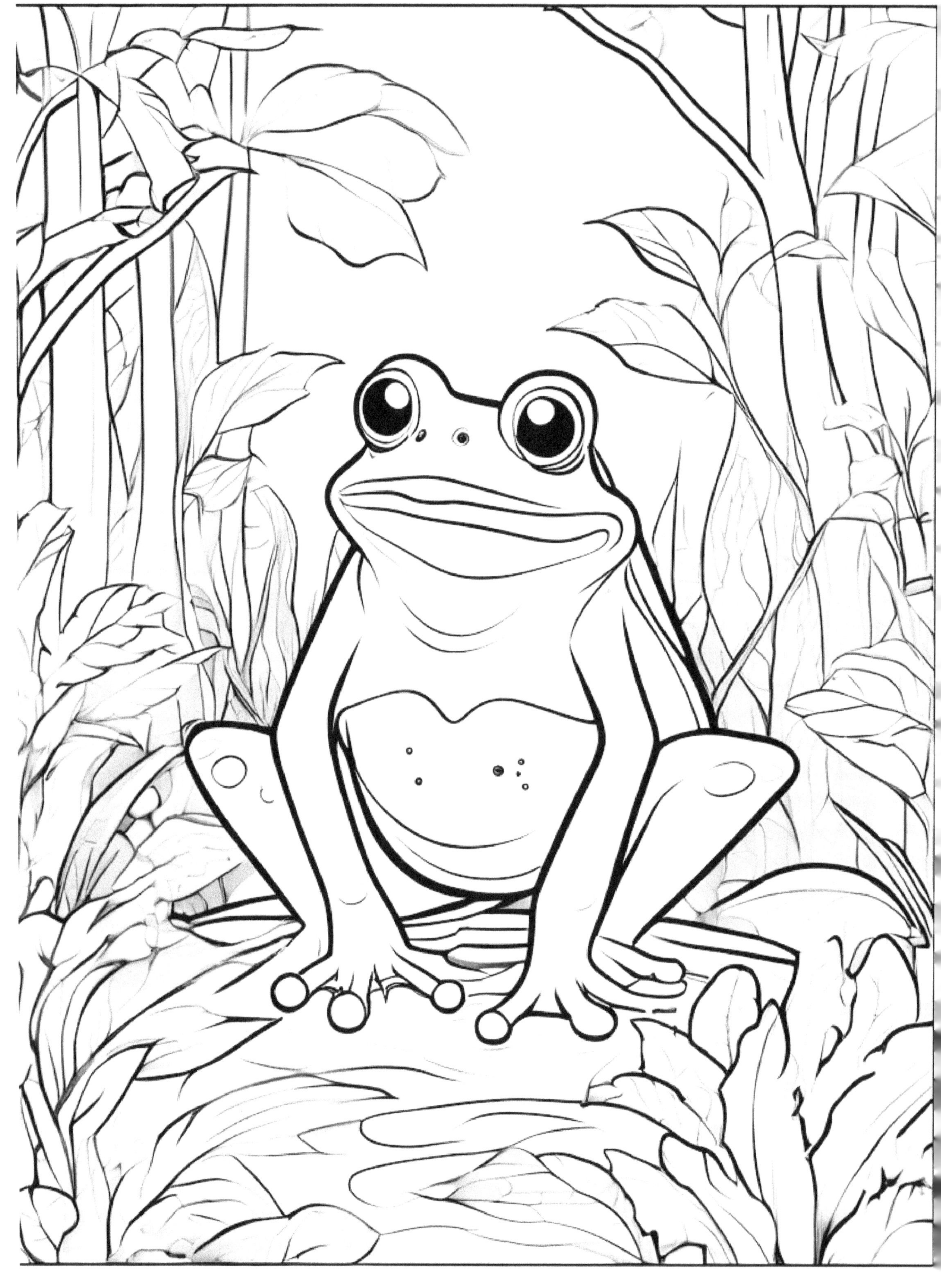

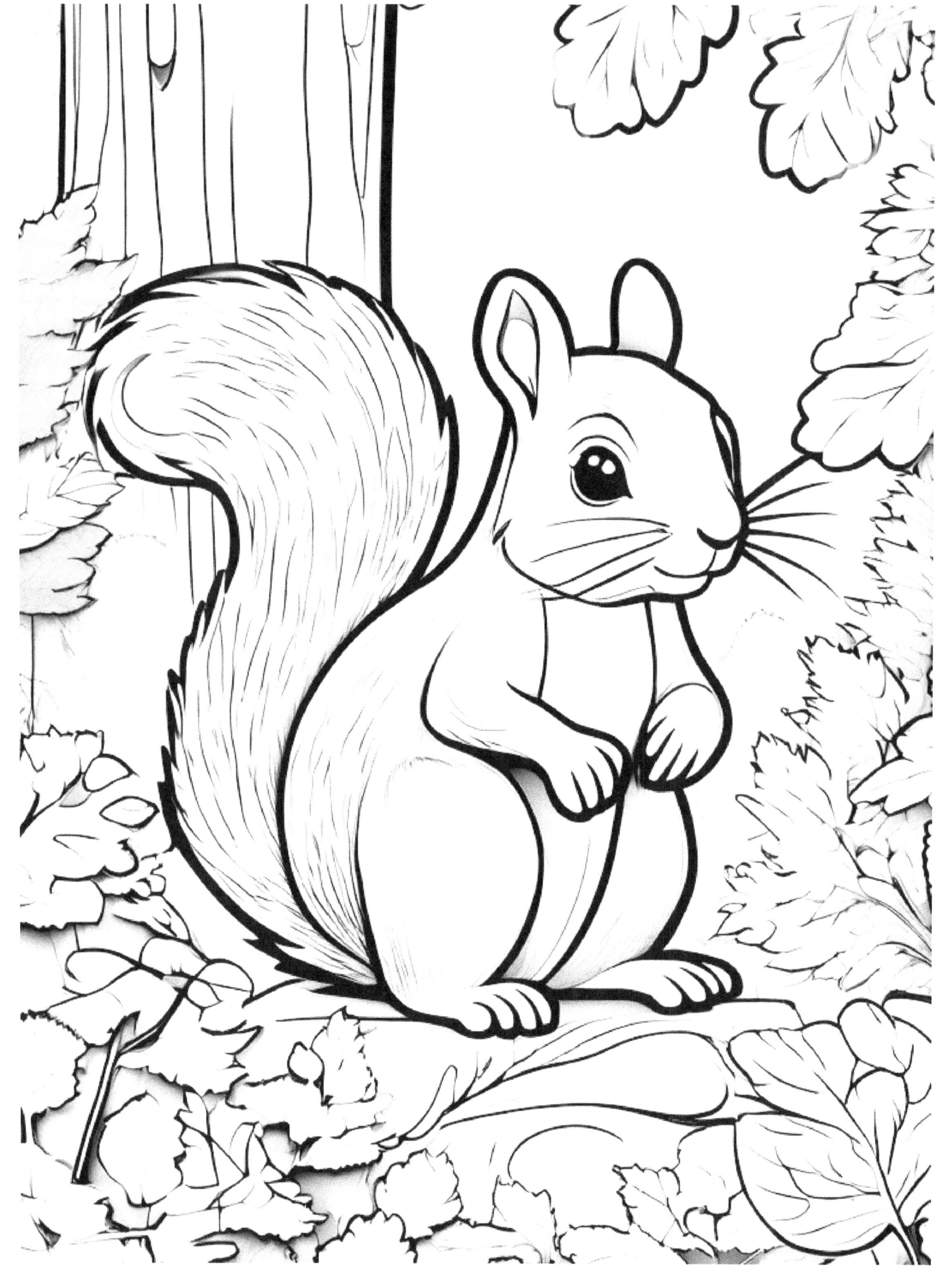

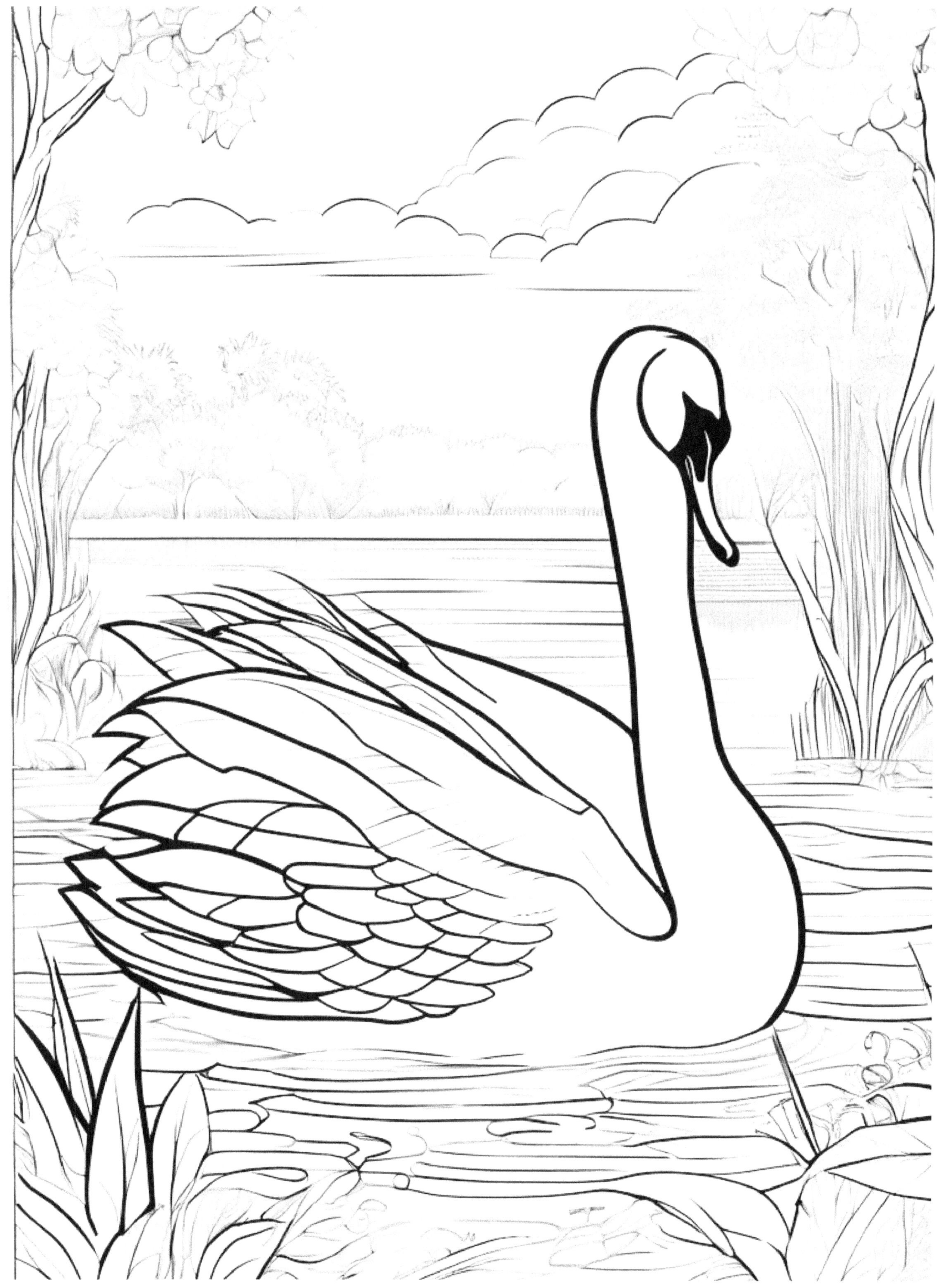

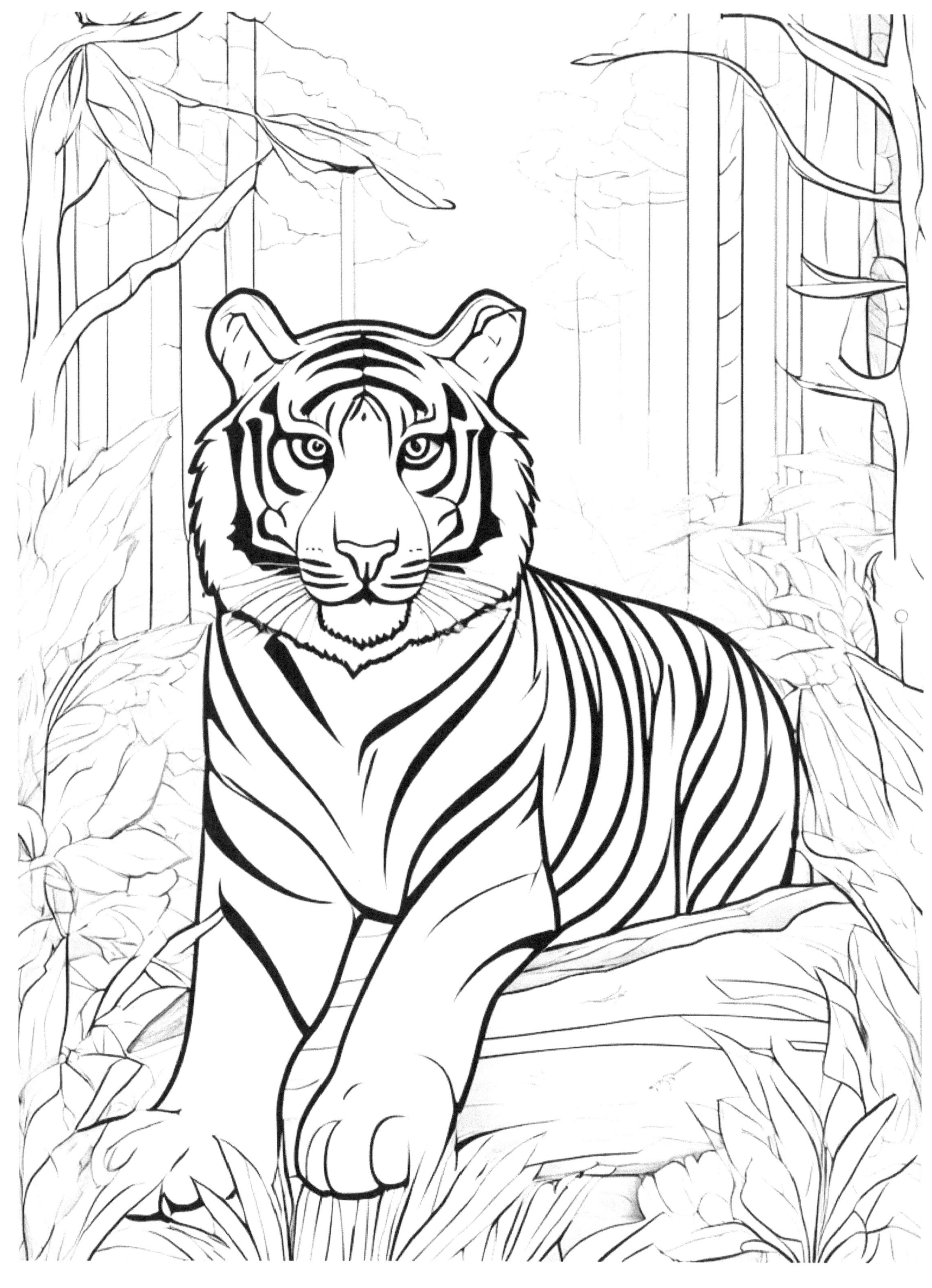

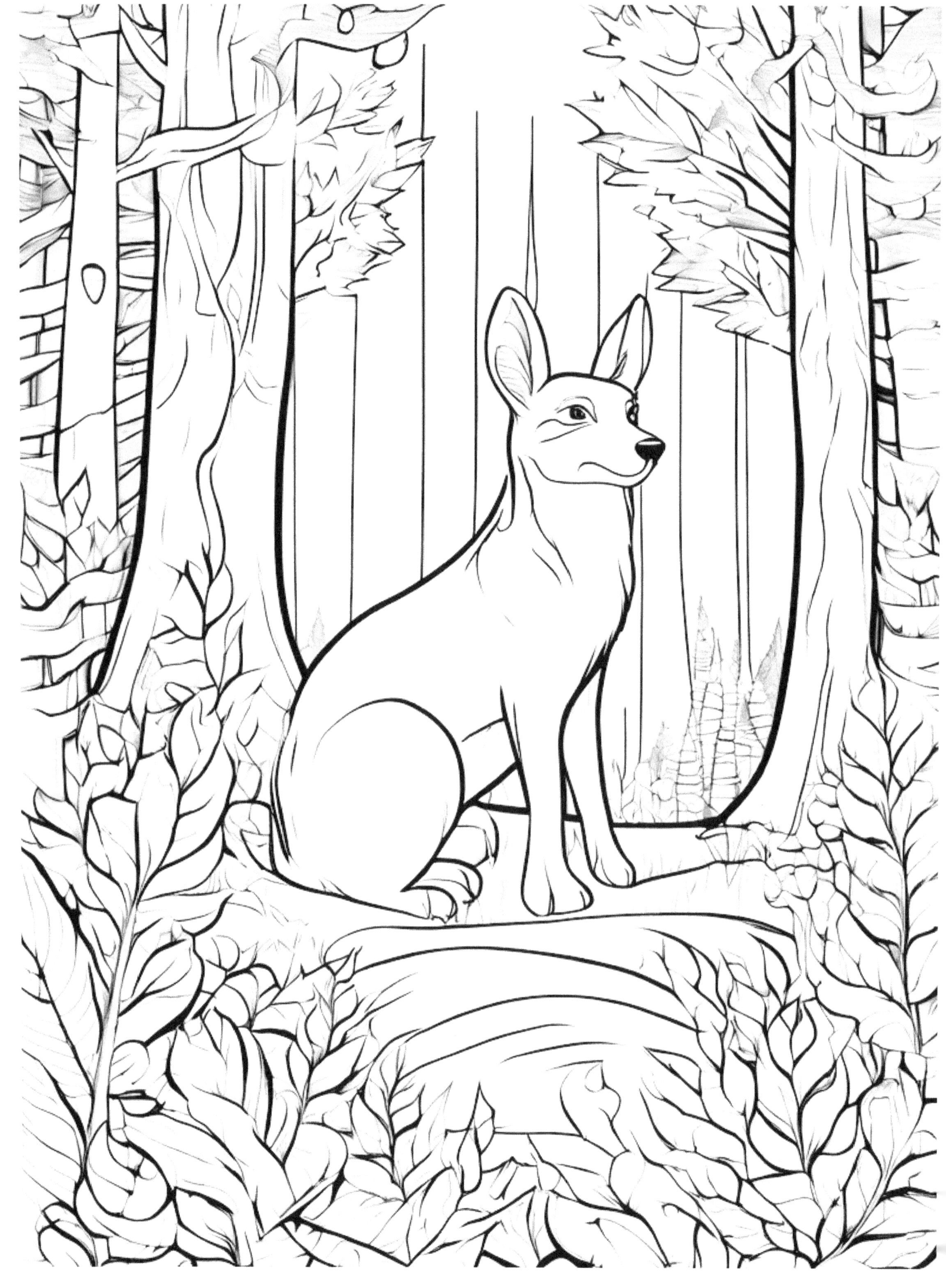

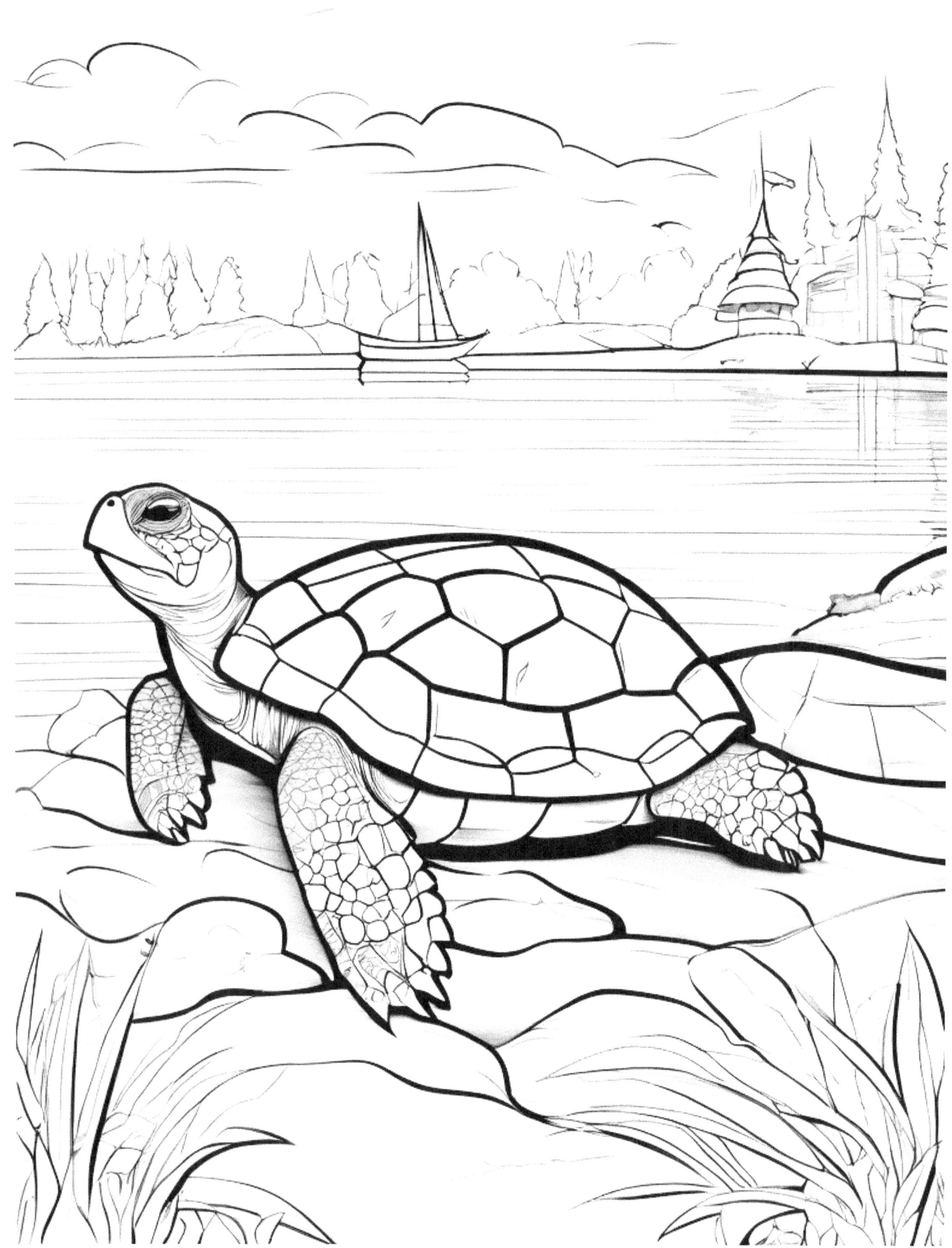

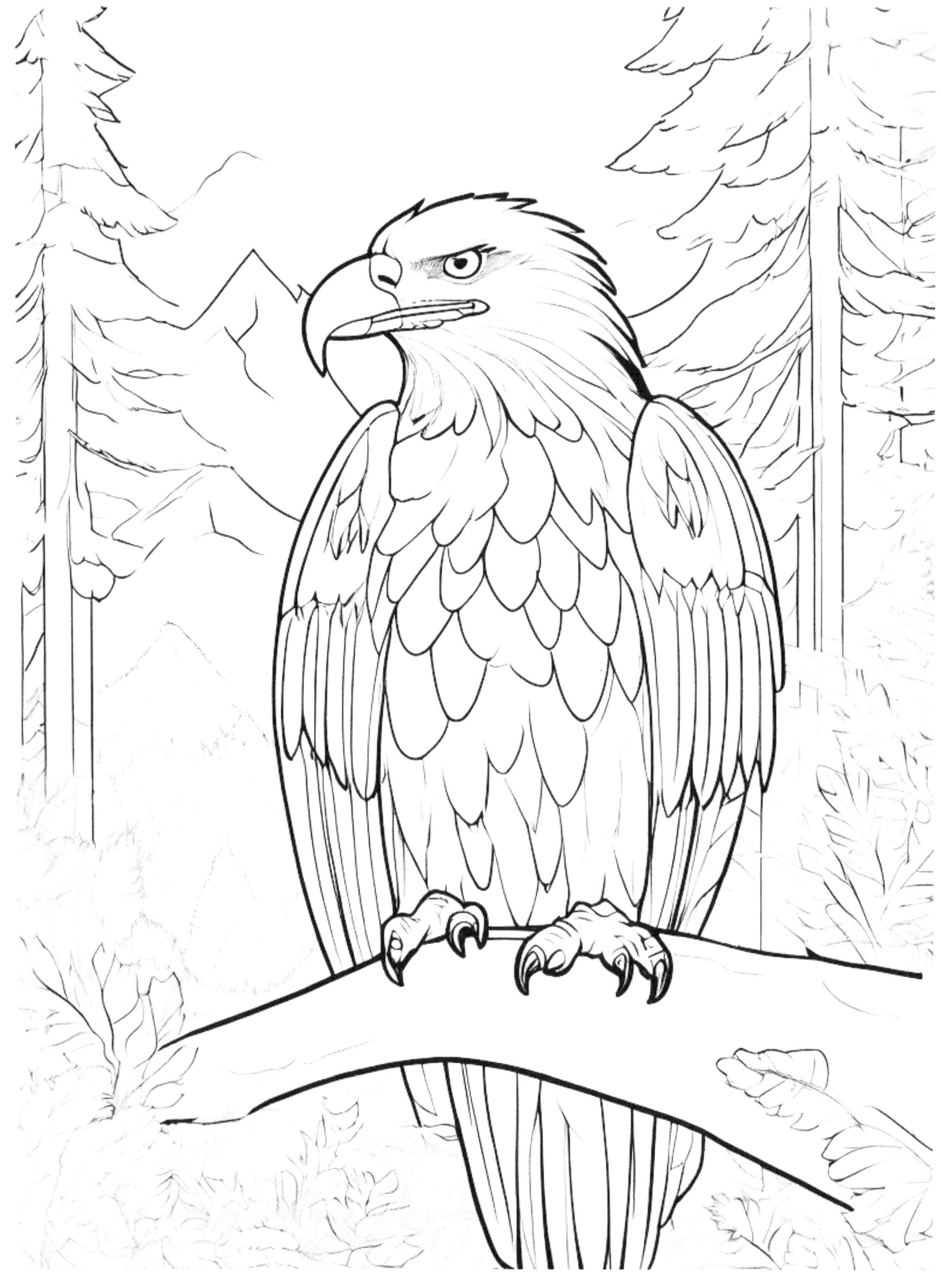

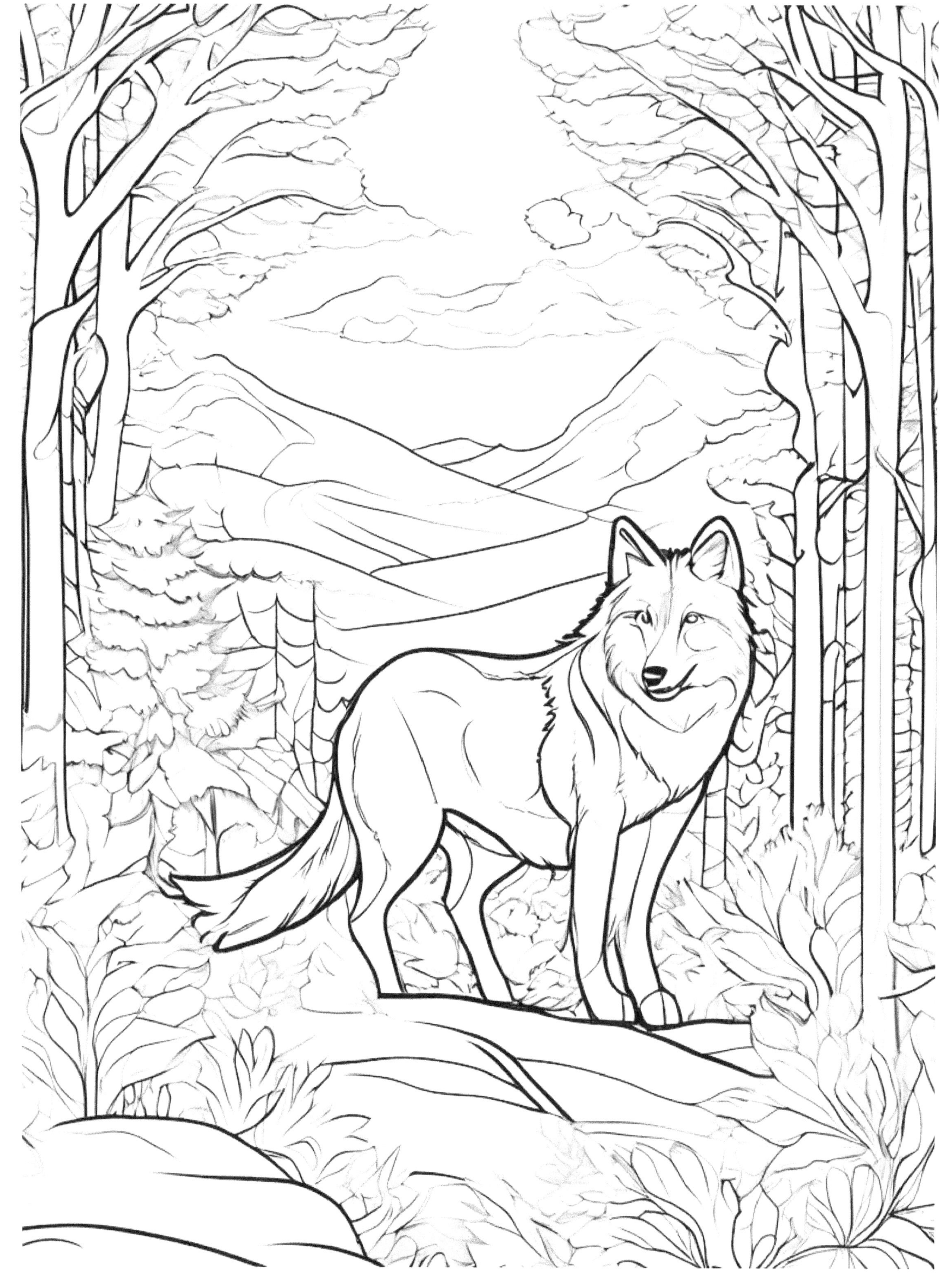

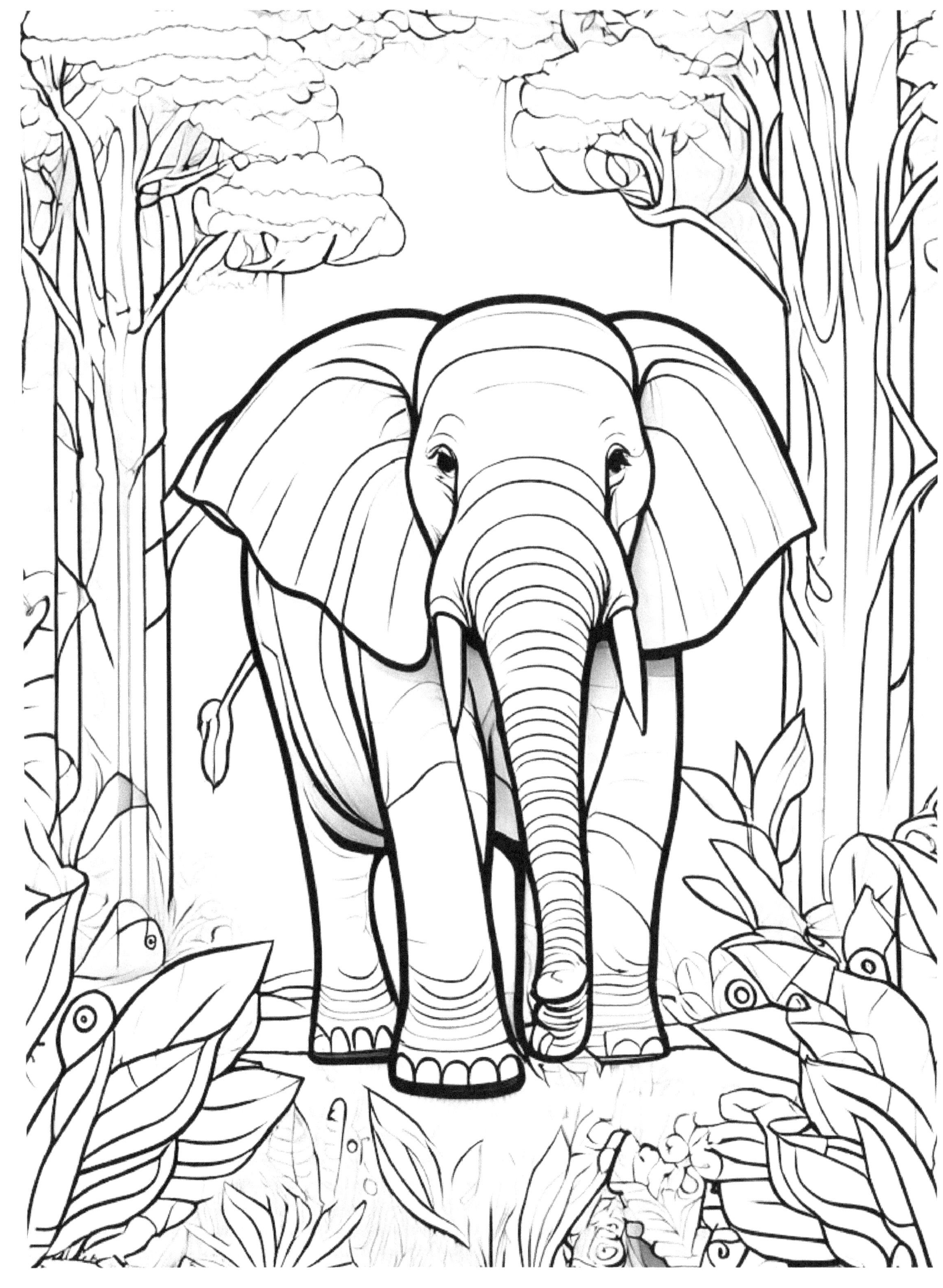

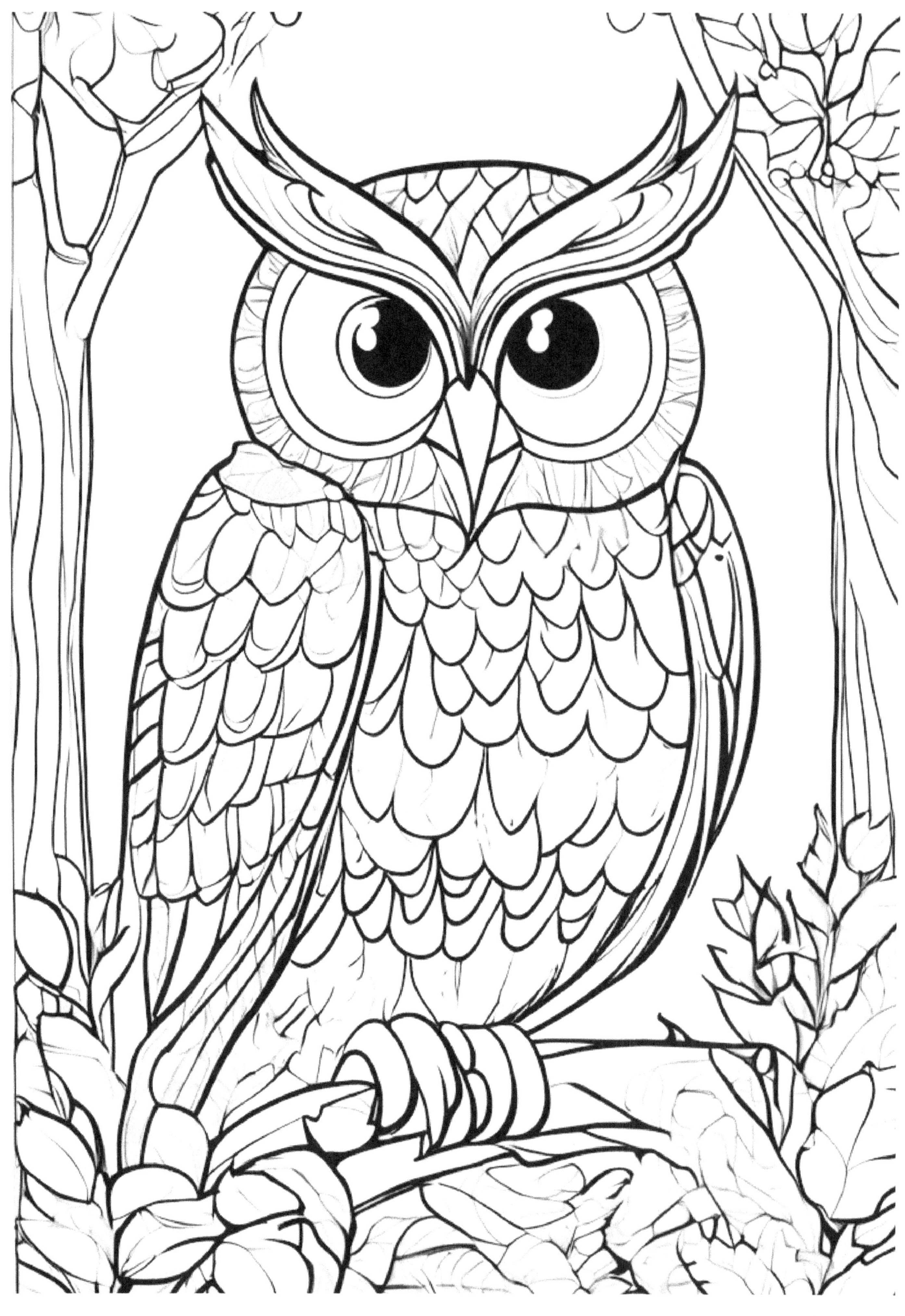

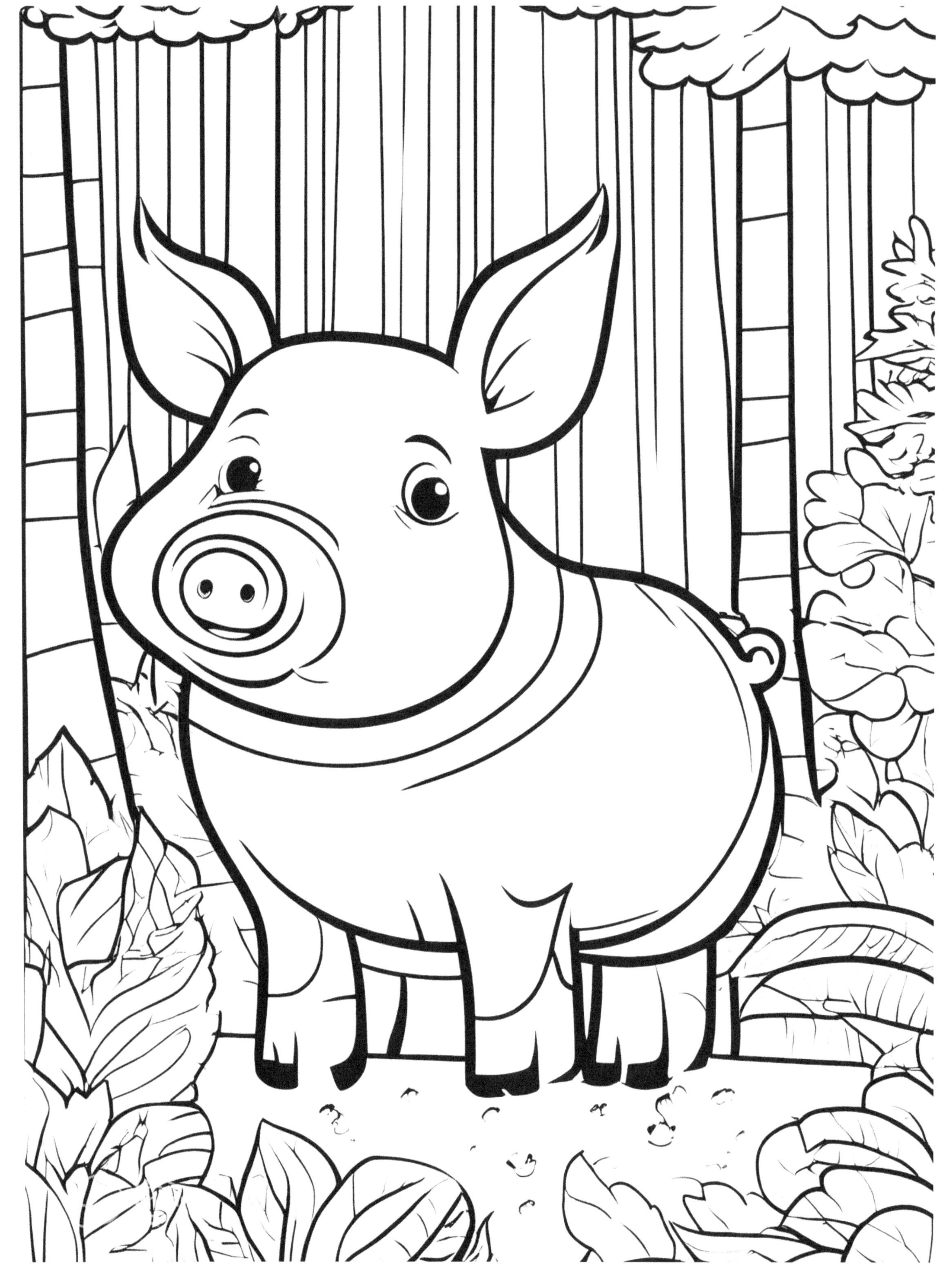

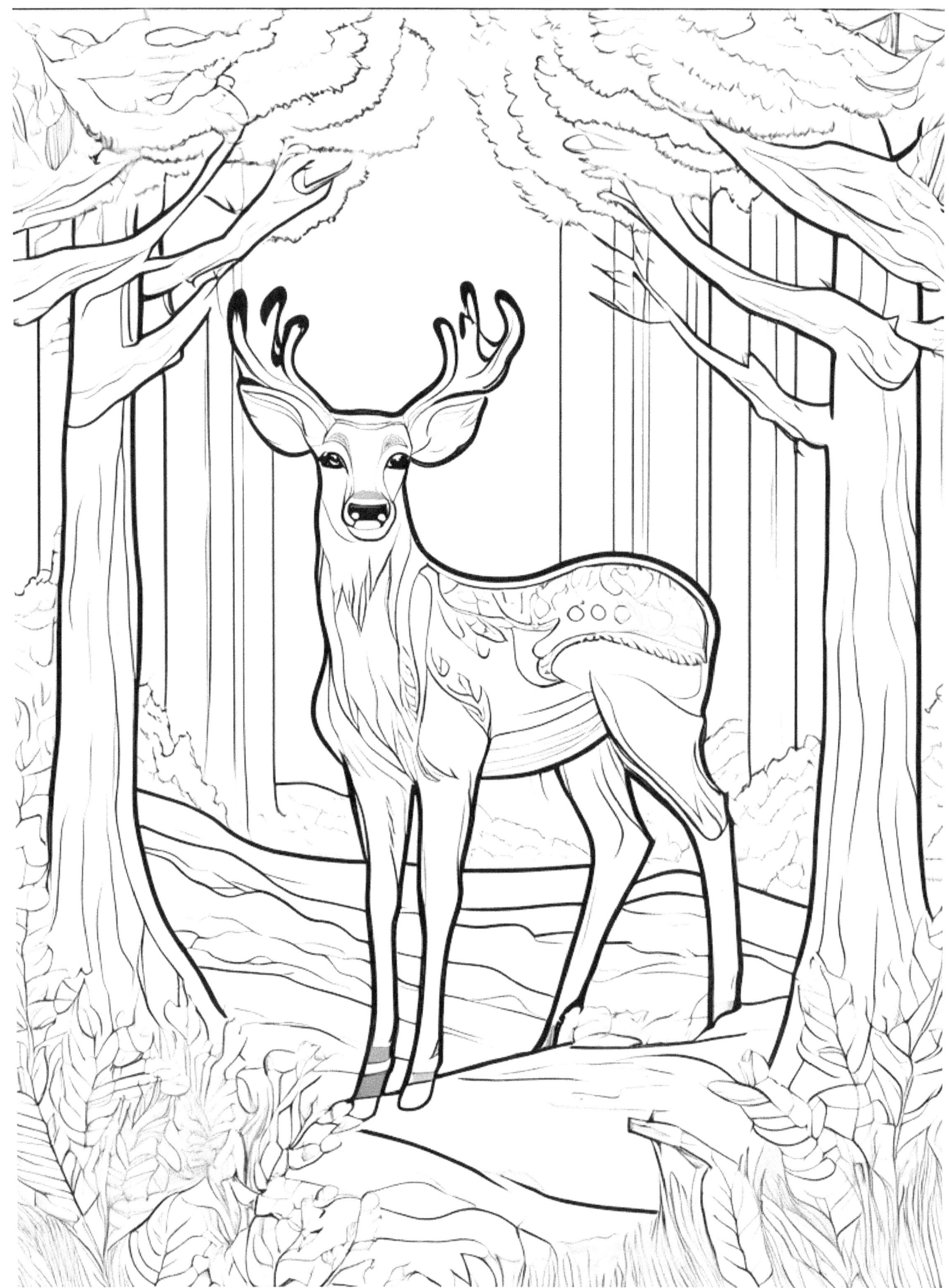